Home Library

EDITOR: Maryanne Blacker

FOOD EDITOR: Pamela Clark

• • •

DESIGNER: Robbylee Phelan

• • •

DEPUTY FOOD EDITOR: Jan Castorina

ASSISTANT FOOD EDITOR: Kathy Snowball

ASSOCIATE FOOD EDITOR: Enid Morrison

SENIOR HOME ECONOMISTS: Alexandra McCowan, Louise Patniotis, Kathy Wharton

HOME ECONOMISTS: Cynthia Black, Leisel Chen, Tracey Kern, Jill Lange, Kathy McGarry, Maggie Quickenden, Dimitra Stais

EDITORIAL COORDINATOR: Elizabeth Hooper

KITCHEN ASSISTANT: Amy Wong

• • •

STYLISTS: Lucy Andrews, Marie-Helene Clauzon, Rosemary de Santis, Carolyn Fienberg, Jane Hann, Jacqui Hing

PHOTOGRAPHERS: Kevin Brown, Robert Clark, Robert Taylor, Jon Waddy

• • •

HOME LIBRARY STAFF

ART DIRECTOR: Paula Wooller

EDITORIAL COORDINATOR: Fiona Nicholas

• • •

PUBLISHER: Richard Walsh

DEPUTY PUBLISHER: Nick Chan

• • •

Produced by The Australian Women's Weekly Home Library. Typeset by ACP Color Graphics, Sydney. Printed by Times Printers Pte. Ltd, Singapore. Published by ACP Publishing, 54 Park Street, Sydney.

• • •

♦ USA: Distributed for Whitecap Books Ltd by Graphic Arts Center Publishing, 3019 N.W. Yeon, Portland, OR, 97210. Tel: 503-226-2402. Fax: 530-223-1410

♦ CANADA: Distributed in Canada by Whitecap Books Ltd, 1086 West 3rd St, North Vancouver B.C. V7P 3J6. Tel: 604-980-9852. Fax: 604-980-8097

• • •

Includes index.
ISBN 1 86396 007 4.

• • •

• • •

COVER: Clockwise from lower right on front cover: Split Pea Soup with Spiced Yogurt, page 13, Vegetable Terrine, page 10, Chicken Roasted with Garlic, page 29, Sago Apple Pie, page 105, Wheatmeal Rolls, page 110, Lamb Shanks with Tomato Basil Sauce, page 57.
OPPOSITE: Individual Rum Babas, page 120.
INSIDE BACK COVER: Quail with Chestnut Seasoning and Grapes, page 20.

COUNTRY COOKING

Comforting, warm, wintry food that evokes the image of good eating in a farmhouse kitchen is all here in recipes with our up-to-date touch. We like the traditional styles of cooking in the pot and in the oven, because they are truly fuss-free; a large percentage of main courses are make-ahead casseroles and hearty roasts that are so easy to serve. To tempt you further, there are hot, luscious desserts and a wonderful baking section with superb breads, rolls and more.

Pamela Clark

FOOD EDITOR

Soups & Terrines

Wonderfully flavored, our thick, hearty soups and interesting terrines would be a big hit as starters, appetizers or lunch dishes; serve them with a salad and crusty bread for extra satisfaction. Most of the soups and all the terrines can be prepared ahead, a great help when you're in a hurry.

TOFU AND GINGERROOT SOUP WITH NOODLES

3oz capellini egg noodles
10oz package firm tofu
2 stalks celery
4 green onions
4 teaspoons Oriental sesame oil
4 teaspoons olive oil
3 cloves garlic, minced
4 teaspoons grated fresh gingerroot
2 tablespoons finely chopped fresh lemon grass
10 pearl onions, quartered
3 tablespoons fresh lemon juice
4 teaspoons light soy sauce
¾ cup canned sliced bamboo shoots, drained
3½ cups vegetable broth
¼ cup shredded fresh basil

Add noodles to large pan of boiling water, boil, uncovered, until tender; drain. Cut tofu into ¾ inch cubes. Cut celery and green onions into 1½ inch lengths.

Heat oils in pan, add garlic, gingerroot, lemon grass and pearl onions, cook, stirring, until onions are soft. Add celery, green onions, juice, sauce and bamboo shoots, cook, stirring, about 5 minutes or until celery is just tender. Add broth, bring to boil, add noodles and tofu, simmer about 3 minutes or until tofu is heated through. Serve sprinkled with basil.

Serves 4 to 6.

■ Recipe best made just before serving.
■ Freeze: Not suitable.
■ Microwave: Noodles suitable.

RIGHT: Tofu and Gingerroot Soup with Noodles.

SPINACH VEGETABLE POTS WITH HERB VINAIGRETTE

¾ bunch (1lb) spinach
1 cup whipping cream

CARROT LAYER
3 large (about 1lb) carrots, chopped
2 eggs
½ teaspoon ground cumin

CAULIFLOWER LAYER
½ medium (about 1lb) cauliflower, chopped
2 eggs

PEA LAYER
1lb package frozen peas, thawed
2 eggs

HERB VINAIGRETTE
⅓ cup olive oil
¼ cup tarragon vinegar
1 clove garlic, minced
½ teaspoon sugar
½ teaspoon seeded mustard
4 teaspoons chopped fresh chives
2 teaspoons chopped fresh thyme

Boil, steam or microwave spinach leaves until just tender; rinse under cold water, drain, pat dry with absorbent paper.

Grease 6 ovenproof dishes (1 cup capacity), line with spinach leaves, allowing leaves to overhang edges. Beat cream in small bowl until soft peaks form.

Divide carrot mixture between dishes, spoon cauliflower mixture over carrot layer; spoon pea mixture over cauliflower layer. Cover with spinach leaves, cover dishes with foil. Place dishes in roasting pan, pour in enough boiling water to come half way up sides of dishes. Bake in 350°F oven about 1¼ hours or until firm; cool. Refrigerate overnight. Serve pots with herb vinaigrette.

Carrot Layer: Boil, steam or microwave carrots until tender; cool. Blend or process carrots, eggs and cumin until smooth. Fold in one-third of the cream.

Cauliflower Layer: Follow carrot layer method as above.

Pea Layer: Follow carrot layer method.

Herb Vinaigrette: Combine all ingredients in jar; shake well.

Makes 6.

- Pots best made a day ahead.
- Storage: Covered, in refrigerator.
- Freeze: Not suitable.
- Microwave: Vegetables suitable.

GAME TERRINE IN PASTRY WITH MARMALADE SAUCE

¼ cup (½ stick) butter
1 medium onion, finely chopped
10oz chicken livers, chopped
2lb rabbit pieces
14oz venison, chopped
¼ cup port wine
½ cup heavy cream
4 teaspoons chopped fresh thyme
2 tablespoons seeded mustard
1½ cups (3½oz) fresh bread crumbs
2 boneless duck breast
    halves, skinned
1 egg, lightly beaten

PASTRY
3 cups (15cz) all-purpose flour
5oz (1¼ sticks) butter, melted
2oz lard, melted
1 egg yolk
½ cup water, approximately

MARMALADE SAUCE
1 cup lime marmalade
2 tablespoons whisky
¼ cup fresh orange juice
¼ cup slivered almonds, toasted

Grease 5½ inch x 8½ inch loaf pan. Heat butter in skillet, add onion and livers, cook, stirring, until onion is soft; cool. Remove rabbit meat from bones; discard bones (you will need about 1½lb rabbit meat for this recipe).

Process rabbit and venison until coarsely chopped. Transfer mixture to bowl, stir in chicken liver mixture, port wine, cream, thyme, mustard and bread crumbs. Cut duck breasts into long strips. Press half the rabbit mixture into prepared pan, top with duck, then remaining rabbit mixture. Cover tightly with greased foil, place on baking sheet, bake in 350°F oven 1½ hours. Remove foil from pan, bake further 20 minutes; cool. Drain excess liquid from terrine, cover, place weight on top of terrine, refrigerate terrine until cold.

Roll pastry to 14 inch square, brush with egg. Place terrine in center of pastry, cut away corners so pastry looks like a large cross. Fold edges of pastry over top of terrine to enclose, trim; press edges together firmly to seal. Place terrine on greased baking sheet, decorate with scraps of pastry. Brush lightly with more egg. Bake in 375°F oven about 40 minutes or until browned; cool. Serve terrine sliced with marmalade sauce.

Pastry: Sift flour into bowl, stir in butter, lard, egg yolk and enough water to mix to a soft dough, cover, refrigerate 1 hour.
Marmalade Sauce: Combine marmalade, whisky and juice in pan, stir over heat, without boiling, until marmalade is melted; cool. Stir in nuts, cover, refrigerate until cold.

Serves 8.

■ Recipe can be made 3 days ahead.
■ Storage: Covered, in refrigerator.
■ Freeze: Not suitable.
■ Microwave: Marmalade sauce suitable.

MUSHROOM SOUP WITH PASTRY LID

3 slices white bread
2 tablespoons (¼ stick) butter
1lb large flat mushrooms, chopped
1 clove garlic, minced
3½ cups vegetable broth
¼ teaspoon ground nutmeg
1¼ cups heavy cream
3 tablespoons chopped fresh parsley
2 sheets (10in x 10in) ready rolled
    puff pastry
1 egg yolk

Remove crusts from bread, break bread into pieces.

Heat butter in pan, add mushrooms and garlic, cook, stirring, until mushrooms are soft. Add bread, broth and nutmeg, simmer, uncovered, 15 minutes. Blend or process mushroom mixture until smooth. Stir in cream and parsley.

Divide soup between 4 ovenproof soup bowls (1 cup capacity), top bowls with pastry, trim edges. Brush top of pastry with egg yolk, place bowls on baking sheet. Bake in 375°F oven about 10 minutes or until pastry is golden brown and puffed.

Serves 4.

■ Soup can be made a day ahead.
■ Storage: Covered, in refrigerator
■ Freeze: Not suitable.
■ Microwave: Soup suitable.

LEFT: From back: Game Terrine in Pastry with Marmalade Sauce, Spinach Vegetable Pots with Herb Vinaigrette.
ABOVE: Mushroom Soup with Pastry Lid.

PASTA AND BEEF SOUP

4 teaspoons olive oil
1lb top sirloin steak, thinly sliced
2 cloves garlic, minced
4 teaspoons olive oil, extra
1 medium onion, chopped
1 clove garlic, minced, extra
1 medium carrot, chopped
1 stalk celery, chopped
½lb button mushrooms, sliced
14½oz can tomatoes
6 cups beef broth
2 cups water
¾ cup small elbow macaroni pasta
2 tablespoons chopped fresh basil
⅓ cup grated Parmesan cheese

Heat oil in skillet, add steak and garlic, cook, stirring, until steak is well browned all over; drain.

Heat extra oil in pan, add onion, extra garlic, carrot and celery, cook, stirring, until vegetables are soft. Add mushrooms, cook, stirring, until lightly browned. Stir in undrained crushed tomatoes, broth and water, bring to boil. Stir in pasta, boil, uncovered, until pasta is tender. Add steak and basil, stir until heated through. Serve soup sprinkled with cheese.

Serves 6.

- Recipe can be made a day ahead.
- Storage: Covered, in refrigerator.
- Freeze: Suitable.
- Microwave: Not suitable.

LENTIL AND SPINACH SOUP

1 cup (7oz) brown lentils
2 bay leaves
1 stalk celery, finely chopped
2 teaspoons grated fresh gingerroot
8 cups chicken broth
1 tablespoon butter
1 large red onion, finely chopped
2 cloves garlic, minced
2 medium ripe tomatoes,
    peeled, chopped
1 bunch (1¼lb) spinach, chopped
2 teaspoons cider vinegar
1 teaspoon chopped fresh cilantro

Combine lentils, bay leaves, celery, gingerroot and broth in large pan, simmer, uncovered, about 30 minutes or until lentils are just soft.

Heat butter in pan, add onion and garlic, cook, stirring, until onion is soft. Add tomatoes, cook, stirring, until tomatoes are pulpy. Add spinach, stir over heat until spinach is wilted. Add spinach mixture to lentil mixture, stir in vinegar and cilantro; stir until heated through. Discard bay leaves before serving.

Serves 6.

- Recipe can be made a day ahead.
- Storage: Covered, in refrigerator.
- Freeze: Suitable.
- Microwave: Suitable.

RED BELL PEPPER SOUP WITH POLENTA

6 (about 3lb) red bell peppers
3 tablespoons olive oil
2 medium (about 10oz) onions,
    chopped
2 cloves garlic, minced
1 teaspoon chopped fresh thyme
4 cups chicken broth
2 teaspoons balsamic vinegar
¼ teaspoon sugar

POLENTA
2 cups chicken broth
½ cup yellow cornmeal
¼ cup grated Parmesan cheese
1 egg yolk
oil for deep-frying

Quarter peppers, remove seeds and membranes. Broil peppers, skin-side-up, until skin blisters and blackens. Peel away skin, chop peppers roughly.

Heat oil in pan, add onions and garlic, cook, stirring, until onions are soft. Add peppers, thyme and broth, simmer, covered, about 10 minutes or until peppers are soft. Stir in vinegar and sugar.

Blend soup in batches until smooth. Return soup to pan, stir until heated through. Serve with polenta.

Polenta: Lightly grease 3½ inch x 10½ inch baking pan. Bring broth to boil in pan, add cornmeal, simmer, uncovered, about 15 minutes, stirring occasionally, or until cornmeal is soft; cool 2 minutes. Stir in cheese and egg yolk, press mixture into prepared pan, cover, refrigerate until cold.

Turn polenta out of pan, cut into ½ inch x 3 inch sticks. Deep-fry polenta sticks in batches in hot oil until lightly browned; drain on absorbent paper.

Serves 4.

- Recipe can be made a day ahead.
- Storage: Covered, in refrigerator.
- Freeze: Soup suitable.
- Microwave: Soup suitable.

LEFT: Clockwise from top: Pasta and Beef Soup, Red Bell Pepper Soup with Polenta, Lentil and Spinach Soup.

HEARTY WINTER BORSCH

10 medium (about 2½lb) beets
3oz (¾ stick) butter
4 cloves garlic, minced
1 large (about 1¼lb) leek, thinly sliced
½lb chopped lean lamb
3 cups (about ½lb) shredded
   cabbage
¼ cup sugar
½ teaspoon ground cloves
2 bay leaves
¼ cup chopped fresh dill
8 cups beef broth
3 tablespoons white vinegar
¾ cup sour cream
1 egg yolk
2 tablespoons chopped
   fresh dill, extra

Peel and grate beets. Heat butter in pan, add beets, garlic, leek and lamb, cook, stirring, until leek is soft. Add cabbage, sugar, cloves, bay leaves, dill, broth and vinegar, simmer, uncovered, about 1 hour or until beets are tender. Remove and discard lamb and bay leaves.

Combine sour cream, yolk and extra dill in bowl. Top borsch with cream mixture.

Serves 8.

■ Soup can be made 2 days ahead. Sour cream topping best made just before serving.
■ Storage: Covered, in refrigerator.
■ Freeze: Not suitable.
■ Microwave: Suitable.

PEA AND HAM SOUP

1½lb ham bone
1 medium onion, chopped
2 cups (10oz) yellow split peas
2 stalks celery, chopped
2 medium carrots, chopped
2 bay leaves
10 cups water

Combine all ingredients in pan, simmer, covered, about 1½ hours or until peas are soft, stirring occasionally.

Remove ham bone, remove ham from bone, chop ham finely; discard bone. Return ham to pan, stir until heated through; discard bay leaves.

Serves 6.

■ Recipe can be made 4 days ahead.
■ Storage: Covered, in refrigerator.
■ Freeze: Suitable.
■ Microwave: Not suitable.

BELOW: Hearty Winter Borsch.
RIGHT: Clockwise from left: Fresh Tomato and Garlic Soup, Pea and Ham Soup, Garbanzo Bean, Spinach and Mushroom Soup.

FRESH TOMATO AND GARLIC SOUP

6 large (about 3lb) ripe tomatoes,
   peeled, seeded
1 tablespoon butter
2 medium onions, finely chopped
4 cloves garlic, minced
1 teaspoon grated fresh gingerroot
2 tablespoons all-purpose flour
2 cups chicken broth
2 tablespoons tomato paste
2 teaspoons sugar
1 teaspoon chopped fresh oregano
1 teaspoon chopped fresh thyme
3 tablespoons chopped fresh parsley

PARMESAN TOAST
1 small French bread stick
¼ cup (½ stick) butter, softened
½ cup grated Parmesan cheese

Blend or process tomatoes until smooth. Heat butter in pan, add onions, garlic and gingerroot, cook, stirring, until onions are soft. Add flour, stir until combined. Remove from heat, gradually stir in tomatoes, broth, paste and sugar, simmer, uncovered, about 15 minutes or until slightly thickened; stir in herbs. Serve with Parmesan toast.

Parmesan Toast: Cut bread into 1¼ inch slices. Combine butter and cheese in bowl, spread mixture evenly over bread, broil until cheese is melted.

Serves 4.

■ Soup can be made 2 days ahead. Parmesan toast best made just before serving.
■ Storage: Covered, in refrigerator.
■ Freeze: Soup suitable.
■ Microwave: Soup suitable.

GARBANZO BEAN, SPINACH AND MUSHROOM SOUP

4 teaspoons olive oil
1 small red onion, chopped
10oz button mushrooms, sliced
14½oz can tomatoes
15oz can tomato puree
1lb can garbanzo beans,
   rinsed, drained
4 cups vegetable broth
2 tablespoons chopped fresh parsley
1 teaspoon seasoned pepper
1 bunch (1¼lb) spinach, shredded

Heat oil in pan, add onion and mushrooms, cook, stirring, until onion is soft. Add undrained crushed tomatoes, puree, garbanzo beans, broth, parsley and pepper, simmer, uncovered, 20 minutes. Add spinach, stir until heated through.

Serves 4 to 6.

■ Recipe can be made a day ahead.
■ Storage: Covered, in refrigerator.
■ Freeze: Not suitable.
■ Microwave: Suitable.

VEGETABLE TERRINE WITH TOMATO SAUCE

1 large (about 1lb) eggplant,
    thinly sliced
coarse (kosher) salt
¼ cup olive oil
2 medium (about 10oz) red bell peppers
2 medium (about 10oz) yellow
    bell peppers
1 bunch (1¼lb) spinach
1 cup (3½oz) shredded
    mozzarella cheese
¼ cup drained sun-dried
    tomatoes, sliced

DOUGH
2 cups all-purpose flour
1 package (¼oz) active dry yeast
1 teaspoon sugar
4 teaspoons olive oil
¾ cup warm water

PESTO
2 cups lightly packed basil leaves
¼ cup pine nuts
2 cloves garlic, minced
⅓ cup olive oil
½ cup grated Parmesan cheese

TOMATO SAUCE
4 teaspoons olive oil
1 medium onion, chopped
2 cloves garlic, minced
14½oz can tomatoes
2 tablespoons chopped fresh basil
¼ teaspoon sugar

Grease 4½ inch x 9 inch loaf dish (6 cup capacity). Sprinkle eggplant with salt, stand 20 minutes. Rinse eggplant under cold water, drain, pat dry with absorbent paper. Heat oil in skillet, cook eggplant until browned; drain on absorbent paper.

Quarter peppers, remove seeds and membranes. Broil peppers, skin-side-up, until skin blisters and blackens. Peel away skins, discard skins. Add spinach to pan of boiling water, drain immediately, rinse under cold water; drain, pat dry with absorbent paper.

Roll three-quarters of the dough large enough to line base and sides of prepared dish, leaving ¾ inch of dough overhanging edges. Sprinkle half the cheese over base of dough, top with eggplant slices, red bell peppers, pesto, yellow bell peppers, spinach, sun-dried tomatoes and remaining cheese.

Roll remaining dough large enough to cover top of dish, brush edges with water, place dough on top; trim edges. Pinch edges together, decorate with dough leaves, if desired. Cut 3 slits in dough, bake in 375°F oven about 40 minutes or until browned. Cool in dish, cut when cold. Serve with tomato sauce.

Dough: Sift flour into bowl, stir in yeast, sugar, oil and water; mix to a firm dough. Knead about 5 minutes on floured surface until smooth and elastic.

Pesto: Blend or process basil, nuts, garlic and oil until smooth; stir in cheese.

Tomato Sauce: Heat oil in pan, add onion and garlic, cook, stirring, until onion is soft. Stir in undrained crushed tomatoes, basil and sugar, simmer, uncovered, 5 minutes or until slightly thickened.

Serves 8.

- Recipe can be made 2 days ahead.
- Storage: Covered, in refrigerator.
- Freeze: Not suitable.
- Microwave: Not suitable.

RABBIT AND VEAL TERRINE WITH TARRAGON MAYONNAISE

4 teaspoons olive oil
2lb rabbit pieces
1 medium onion, chopped
1 clove garlic, minced
½ cup dry white wine
2 medium carrots, finely chopped
2 stalks celery, finely chopped
¼ cup unflavored gelatin
½ cup water
⅔ cup chopped fresh parsley
4 teaspoons chopped fresh thyme
4 teaspoons chopped fresh tarragon

VEAL BROTH
4lb veal bones
20 cups water
2 medium onions, chopped
2 stalks celery, chopped
2 medium carrots, chopped
3 bay leaves
2 teaspoons black peppercorns

TARRAGON MAYONNAISE
3 egg yolks
1 clove garlic, minced
2 tablespoons fresh lemon juice
1½ cups vegetable oil
1 teaspoon chopped fresh tarragon

Heat oil in pan, add rabbit, cook until browned all over. Transfer rabbit to ovenproof dish. Add onion and garlic to same pan, cook, stirring, until onion is soft, stir in wine and 2 cups of veal broth; bring to boil. Pour broth mixture over rabbit, cover, bake in 350°F oven about 1½ hours or until rabbit is tender.

Drain rabbit, discard liquid. Remove meat from bones, chop meat finely; discard bones.

Bring 5 cups veal broth to boil in pan, add carrots and celery, simmer, uncovered, 5 minutes or until vegetables are tender; cool slightly.

Sprinkle gelatin over water in cup, stand in pan of simmering water, stir until dissolved. Stir gelatin mixture into broth mixture. Mixture should be partly set before using. Stir 1 cup partly set broth mixture into rabbit.

Oil 4½ inch x 10 inch loaf dish (6 cup capacity). Spoon one-third of the remaining broth mixture into prepared dish, sprinkle with half the combined parsley, thyme and tarragon. Place half the rabbit mixture over herbs, repeat layering, ending with broth mixture. Cover dish, refrigerate overnight. Serve terrine with tarragon mayonnaise.

Veal Broth: Combine all ingredients in large pan, simmer, uncovered, 3 hours. Strain broth, discard bones and vegetables. Refrigerate broth overnight. Skim fat from broth. You will need 7 cups broth for this recipe.

Tarragon Mayonnaise: Blend egg yolks, garlic and juice until smooth. Add oil gradually in a thin stream while motor is operating; stir in tarragon.

Serves 8.

- ▧ Recipe can be made 2 days ahead.
- ▧ Storage: Covered, in refrigerator.
- ▧ Freeze: Not suitable.
- ▧ Microwave: Gelatin suitable.

LEFT: Vegetable Terrine with Tomato Sauce.
RIGHT: Rabbit and Veal Terrine with Tarragon Mayonnaise.

BACON AND VEGETABLE SOUP WITH BARLEY

2lb bacon bones
1 bay leaf
1 sprig fresh thyme
1 sprig fresh parsley
4 black peppercorns
4 teaspoons olive oil
1 medium onion, chopped
2 medium carrots, chopped
2 stalks celery, chopped
8 cups water
1/3 cup pearl barley

Add bacon bones to large pan of cold water; bring to boil, strain bacon bones, rinse bones under cold water; pat dry with absorbent paper.

Tie bay leaf, herbs and peppercorns in small piece of muslin. Heat oil in pan, add bacon bones, cook until well browned. Add muslin bag, onion, carrots, celery and water, simmer, covered, 2 hours. Remove bacon bones from soup, remove bacon from bones; chop bacon, discard bones. Return bacon to soup, bring soup to boil, add barley, simmer, uncovered, about 40 minutes or until barley is tender. Discard muslin bag; cool soup. Cover soup, refrigerate overnight. Skim fat from soup before reheating.

Serves 4.

- Recipe best made a day ahead.
- Storage: Covered, in refrigerator.
- Freeze: Suitable.
- Microwave: Not suitable.

SPLIT PEA SOUP WITH SPICED YOGURT

2 cups (11oz) yellow split peas
4 teaspoons olive oil
1 small leek, sliced
1 medium onion, sliced
1 clove garlic, minced
2 teaspoons grated fresh gingerroot
1 teaspoon ground cumin
3/4 cup frozen whole-kernel corn
2 stalks celery, chopped
1 large carrot, chopped
3 tablespoons chopped fresh parsley
10 cups vegetable broth
2 teaspoons Worcestershire sauce
2 tablespoons chopped fresh parsley, extra

SPICED YOGURT
2/3 cup plain yogurt
1/2 teaspoon celery salt
1/4 teaspoon ground cumin
1/8 teaspoon cayenne pepper

Cover peas with water in bowl, stand 2 hours. Drain peas, rinse under cold water, drain well.

Heat oil in pan, add leek, onion and garlic, cook, stirring, until onion is soft. Add gingerroot and cumin, cook, stirring, 1 minute. Add peas, corn, celery, carrot, parsley, broth and sauce, simmer, uncovered, 2 hours, skimming occasionally. Serve soup topped with spiced yogurt, sprinkle with extra parsley.
Spiced Yogurt: Combine all ingredients in bowl; mix well.

Serves 6.

- Recipe can be made 2 days ahead.
- Storage: Covered, in refrigerator.
- Freeze: Soup suitable.
- Microwave: Not suitable.

LAMB MEATBALL AND VERMICELLI SOUP

6oz vermicelli
1 stalk celery
1 medium (about 3/4lb) leek
1 small carrot
1 small red bell pepper
1lb ground lamb
1 small onion, chopped
1 clove garlic, minced
4 teaspoons chopped fresh rosemary
2 tablespoons chopped fresh parsley
1/2 teaspoon ground cumin
1 egg, lightly beaten
1/2 cup fresh bread crumbs
3 tablespoons olive oil
7 cups beef broth

Add vermicelli to large pan of boiling water, boil, uncovered, until just tender, drain. Cut celery, leek, carrot and pepper into thin strips about 2 inches long.

Combine lamb, onion, garlic, herbs, cumin, egg and bread crumbs in bowl. Roll rounded tablespoons of mixture into balls. Heat oil in skillet, add meatballs, cook until browned, drain. Bring broth to boil in pan, add vegetables and meatballs, simmer, uncovered, until vegetables are tender. Add vermicelli, stir until hot.

Serves 6.

- Recipe can be made a day ahead.
- Storage: Covered, in refrigerator.
- Freeze: Meatballs suitable.
- Microwave: Vermicelli suitable.

LEFT: From left: Split Pea Soup with Spiced Yogurt, Bacon and Vegetable Soup with Barley. BELOW: Lamb Meatball and Vermicelli Soup.

LAMB AND RAISIN TERRINE

10 slices bacon
¾ cup dark seedless raisins
2 tablespoons (¼ stick) butter
1 medium onion, chopped
2 teaspoons ground cumin
2lb leg of lamb, boned, chopped
2 cups (4½oz) fresh bread crumbs
¾ cup heavy cream
1 teaspoon cracked black
    peppercorns
⅓ cup chopped fresh parsley
½ cup roasted unsalted cashews

Line 4½ inch x 8½ inch loaf dish (6 cup capacity) with bacon, leaving ends of bacon overhanging edges of dish. Place raisins in bowl, cover with boiling water, stand 1 hour; drain.

Heat butter in small skillet, add onion and cumin, cook, stirring, until onion is soft; cool. Process onion mixture, lamb, bread crumbs, cream and pepper in batches until finely ground. Transfer mixture to bowl, stir in drained raisins, parsley and nuts.

Press lamb mixture into prepared dish, fold overhanging bacon over mixture. Cover dish with foil, place in roasting pan with enough boiling water to come halfway up sides of dish. Bake in 350°F oven about 2 hours or until firm; cool. Drain excess liquid from terrine, cover, place weight on top of terrine, refrigerate until cold. Serve sliced.

Serves 6 to 8.

▪ Recipe can be made 4 days ahead.
▪ Storage: Covered, in refrigerator.
▪ Freeze: Not suitable.
▪ Microwave: Not suitable.

PORK ROULADE WITH BELL PEPPER SAUCE

6 large Swiss chard leaves
8 slices (about 6oz) mortadella

PORK FILLING
2 teaspoons olive oil
3 cloves garlic, minced
4 slices bacon, chopped
15oz pork fillets, chopped
¾ cup (1½ sticks) butter, chopped
¼ cup unsalted pistachios
½ small red bell pepper
3 tablespoons chopped fresh basil

BELL PEPPER SAUCE
2 large (about 1¼lb) red bell peppers
1 clove garlic, minced

Boil, steam or microwave Swiss chard until just wilted, rinse under cold water; drain, pat dry with absorbent paper.

Place 12 inch x 16 inch sheet of foil on bench, top with plastic wrap. Layer slices of mortadella, slightly overlapping, on plastic. Spread pork filling evenly over mortadella, top with Swiss chard leaves. Roll up like a jelly-roll, twist ends of foil; refrigerate until firm. Serve pork and spinach roulade with bell pepper sauce.

Pork Filling: Heat oil in skillet, add garlic, bacon and pork, cook, stirring, until pork is tender. Process mixture with butter until smooth. Transfer mixture to bowl, stir in nuts, finely chopped pepper and basil, mix well; cool.

Bell Pepper Sauce: Quarter peppers, remove seeds and membranes, place on baking sheet. Broil peppers, skin-side-up, until skin blisters and blackens. Peel away skin, discard skin, cool peppers. Blend or process peppers and garlic until smooth.

Serves 4 to 6.

▪ Recipe can be made a day ahead.
▪ Storage: Covered, in refrigerator.
▪ Freeze: Bell pepper sauce suitable.
▪ Microwave: Swiss chard suitable.

LEFT: From top: Pork Roulade with Bell Pepper Sauce, Lamb and Raisin Terrine.
ABOVE: Chicken and Corn Chowder.

CHICKEN AND CORN CHOWDER

3½lb boiling chicken
12 cups water
1 medium onion, halved
1 medium carrot, chopped
1 stalk celery, chopped
3 large (about 1¼lb) potatoes,
    chopped
3½ cups canned creamed corn
2 teaspoons chicken bouillon powder
2 teaspoons French mustard
3 tablespoons cornstarch
½ cup half-and-half
2 tablespoons chopped fresh chives

Combine chicken, water, onion, carrot and celery in large pan, simmer, covered, 2 hours. Remove chicken from pan, strain broth; reserve 8 cups broth. Remove skin from chicken, chop chicken; discard skin and bones.

Place reserved broth and potatoes in pan, simmer, covered, until potatoes are tender. Blend or process potato mixture in batches until smooth, return to pan. Add chicken, corn, bouillon powder, mustard and blended cornstarch and half-and-half to pan, stir over heat until soup boils and thickens slightly; stir in chives.

Serves 8.

▪ Recipe can be made a day ahead.
▪ Storage: Covered, in refrigerator.
▪ Freeze: Suitable.
▪ Microwave: Suitable.

TOMATO AND OMELET ROLL SOUP

3½oz sliced prosciutto
3 tablespoons olive oil
1 medium onion, chopped
1 clove garlic, minced
28oz can tomatoes
4 cups beef broth
1 teaspoon sugar
2 tablespoons chopped fresh basil

OMELET ROLLS
¼ cup all-purpose flour
¼ cup grated Parmesan cheese
4 teaspoons chopped fresh basil
3 eggs, lightly beaten
½ cup milk
3 tablespoons butter

Cut prosciutto into thin strips. Heat oil in pan, add onion and garlic, cook, stirring, until onion is soft. Stir in undrained crushed tomatoes, broth and sugar, simmer, covered, about 10 minutes or until tomatoes are soft. Stir in prosciutto, basil and omelet rolls, stir until hot.

Omelet Rolls: Combine flour, cheese and basil in bowl, gradually stir in eggs and milk. Heat 2 teaspoons of the butter in large skillet, pour in ¼ cup egg mixture, cook until browned and set. Turn omelet, brown other side; remove from pan, roll up tightly. Repeat with remaining butter and egg mixture. Cut rolls into ½ inch slices.

Serves 4.

■ Recipe can be prepared a day ahead.
■ Storage: Soup and rolls separately, covered, in refrigerator.
■ Freeze: Soup suitable.
■ Microwave: Soup suitable.

FISH AND LEEK BISQUE WITH GARLIC SOURDOUGH BREAD

1 tablespoon butter
1 medium (about ¾lb) leek, sliced
½ cup dry white wine
¼ cup brandy
2 medium ripe tomatoes, peeled, chopped
⅓ cup short-grain rice
2 tablespoons tomato paste
6 cups fish broth
½ cup heavy cream
2 egg yolks
¾lb boneless white fish fillets, chopped
2 tablespoons chopped fresh dill

GARLIC SOURDOUGH BREAD
½ loaf sourdough bread
⅓ cup olive oil
1 clove garlic, minced

Heat butter in pan, add leek, cook, stirring, until leek is soft. Add wine, brandy, tomatoes, rice, paste and broth, simmer, uncovered, 20 minutes. Stir in combined cream and egg yolks. Blend or process soup in batches until smooth. Return soup to pan, add fish and dill, stir, without boiling, until fish is tender. Serve soup with garlic sourdough bread.

Garlic Sourdough Bread: Cut bread into ½ inch slices. Brush both sides of bread with combined oil and garlic. Place bread in a single layer on baking sheet. Bake in 325°F oven 30 minutes, turn bread, bake further 30 minutes.

Serves 6.

- Soup can be made a day ahead.
- Storage: Covered, in refrigerator.
- Freeze: Not suitable.
- Microwave: Soup suitable.

LAMB SHANKS AND RICE SOUP

4 (about 2lb) lamb shanks
4 teaspoons olive oil
8 cups water
2 tablespoons (¼ stick) butter
1 teaspoon chopped fresh dill
2 tablespoons chopped fresh parsley
3 green onions, chopped
3½oz button mushrooms, sliced
2 tablespoons all-purpose flour
1 medium carrot, chopped
2 tablespoons short-grain rice
½ bunch (about 10oz) spinach, shredded
2 teaspoons fresh lemon juice

Place shanks in roasting pan, brush with oil, bake, uncovered, in 400°F oven about 25 minutes or until well browned. Drain on absorbent paper.

Combine shanks and water in pan, simmer, uncovered, 30 minutes. Remove shanks from pan, reserve 5 cups cooking liquid. Remove lamb from bones, chop lamb and reserve; discard bones.

Heat butter in pan, add herbs, onions and mushrooms, cook, stirring, until mushrooms are soft. Add flour, cook, stirring, until combined. Remove from heat, gradually stir in reserved cooking liquid, carrot and rice, simmer, partly covered, about 12 minutes or until rice is tender.

Add reserved lamb, spinach and juice, stir until spinach is just wilted and soup is heated through.

Serves 4.

- Recipe can be prepared a day ahead.
- Storage: Covered, in refrigerator.
- Freeze: Not suitable.
- Microwave: Not suitable.

LEFT: From back: Fish and Leek Bisque with Garlic Sourdough Bread, Tomato and Omelet Roll Soup.
ABOVE: Lamb Shanks and Rice Soup.

BROAD BEAN SOUP WITH PUMPKIN SQUASH DUMPLINGS

We used fresh broad beans in this recipe; ½lb frozen broad beans can be used instead, if preferred.

¼ cup (½ stick) butter
2 medium (about 1½lb) leeks, sliced
1 clove garlic, minced
2lb ham bones
9 cups water
14½oz can tomatoes
1lb broad beans, shelled
1 cup (¼lb) frozen green peas

PUMPKIN SQUASH DUMPLINGS
½ cup cold mashed pumpkin squash
1 egg, lightly beaten
⅔ cup self-rising flour
⅓ cup grated Parmesan cheese
1 teaspoon seasoned pepper

Heat butter in pan, add leeks and garlic, cook, stirring, until leeks are soft. Add ham bones, water and undrained crushed tomatoes, simmer, covered, 2 hours.

Remove bones from soup, remove ham from bones, chop ham; return ham to soup; discard bones. Cool soup, cover, refrigerate overnight.

Skim fat from soup. Bring soup to boil in pan, add beans and peas. Drop level tablespoons of dumpling mixture into soup, simmer, uncovered, without stirring, about 10 minutes or until dumplings are cooked and vegetables are tender. Turn dumplings once during cooking.

Pumpkin Squash Dumplings: Combine squash and egg in bowl, stir in sifted flour, cheese and pepper.

Serves 6.

- Soup, without dumplings, best made a day ahead.
- Storage: Covered, in refrigerator.
- Freeze: Suitable.
- Microwave: Suitable.

CABBAGE AND BEAN SOUP

¾ cup dried borlotti beans
1 cup (6oz) frozen broad
   beans, thawed
2 tablespoons (¼ stick) butter
1 medium onion, chopped
1 medium (about ¾lb) leek, chopped
1 stalk celery, chopped
2 tablespoons all-purpose flour
8 cups vegetable broth
⅛ teaspoon cayenne pepper
½ teaspoon sugar
¼ teaspoon ground saffron
1 small (about ½lb) sweet
   potato, chopped
3 cups (about ½lb) shredded
   cabbage
3 tablespoons chopped fresh cilantro

Place borlotti beans in bowl, cover with water, cover, stand overnight; drain.

Add broad beans to pan of boiling water, simmer, uncovered, 5 minutes; drain, rinse under cold water. Peel skins from broad beans; discard skins.

Heat butter in pan, add onion, leek and celery, cook, covered, stirring occasionally, about 10 minutes or until vegetables are soft. Add flour, cook, stirring, until mixture is dry and grainy. Remove from heat, gradually stir in broth, pepper, sugar and saffron. Stir over heat until mixture boils and thickens, add borlotti beans, simmer, covered, about 50 minutes or until beans are tender. Add broad beans, sweet potato and cabbage, simmer, uncovered, about 10 minutes or until sweet potato is tender; stir in cilantro.

Serves 6.

- Recipe can be made a day ahead.
- Storage: Covered, in refrigerator.
- Freeze: Not suitable.
- Microwave: Suitable.

CAULIFLOWER AND STILTON SOUP

4 teaspoons olive oil
1 medium onion, sliced
1 medium (about 2lb) cauliflower,
   chopped
5 cups chicken broth
1 cup heavy cream
¼ cup half-and-half
3½oz stilton cheese, crumbled
2oz stilton cheese, crumbled, extra
2 tablespoons chopped fresh chives

Heat oil in large pan, add onion, cook, stirring, until soft. Add cauliflower and broth, simmer, covered, about 25 minutes or until cauliflower is tender. Blend or process soup in batches until smooth. Return soup to pan, stir in cream, half-and-half and cheese, cook, stirring, without boiling, until heated through. Serve soup sprinkled with extra stilton cheese and chopped chives.

Serves 6.

- Recipe can be prepared a day ahead.
- Storage: Covered, in refrigerator.
- Freeze: Not suitable.
- Microwave: Suitable.

RIGHT: Clockwise from left: Cauliflower and Stilton Soup, Broad Bean Soup with Pumpkin Squash Dumplings, Cabbage and Bean Soup.

Poultry

Herbs and spice and all things nice make the best chicken dishes you'll taste anywhere. Here, we offer you delicious classics with fresh style for today, plus new recipes brimming with temptation. For variety, we've included quail, Rock Cornish hens and a very special rolled duck with madeira, bacon and olives.

QUAIL WITH CHESTNUT SEASONING AND GRAPES

6 quail
2 tablespoons olive oil
4 teaspoons olive oil, extra
3 medium (about ¾lb) carrots, chopped
3 medium (about 15oz) onions, chopped
1 bay leaf
1 cup dry red wine
1lb dark grapes
4 teaspoons redcurrant jelly
2 tablespoons cornstarch
2½ cups chicken broth

CHESTNUT SEASONING
2 teaspoons olive oil
2 slices bacon, chopped
⅓ cup canned water chestnuts, drained, chopped
3 tablespoons chopped fresh chives
½ cup cooked white rice
1 egg, lightly beaten

Fill quail with chestnut seasoning, tuck wings under bodies, tie legs together.

Heat oil in flameproof dish, brown quail all over; drain on absorbent paper. Heat extra oil in same dish, add carrots, onions and bay leaf, cook, stirring, until onions are soft; return quail to dish. Bake, uncovered, in 350°F oven about 20 minutes or until quail are tender.

Remove quail and vegetables from dish; keep warm. Place dish over heat, add wine and grapes, simmer, uncovered, until liquid is reduced by about half. Stir in redcurrant jelly and blended cornstarch and broth. Stir over heat until sauce boils and thickens. Serve quail and vegetables with sauce.

Chestnut Seasoning: Heat oil in skillet, add bacon, cook, stirring, until crisp, drain on absorbent paper. Combine bacon with remaining ingredients in bowl; mix well.

Serves 6.

- Recipe can be prepared a day ahead.
- Storage: Covered, in refrigerator.
- Freeze: Not suitable.
- Microwave: Chestnut seasoning suitable.

RIGHT: Quail with Chestnut Seasoning and Grapes.

CHICKEN WITH TARRAGON VINEGAR AND FRESH HERBS

8 chicken thighs, skinned
all-purpose flour
¼ cup vegetable oil
1 medium onion, chopped
1 clove garlic, minced
2 tablespoons chopped fresh
    tarragon
¼ cup tarragon vinegar
¼ cup dry white wine
⅔ cup chicken broth

⅓ cup heavy cream
1 teaspoon chopped fresh parsley
1 teaspoon chopped fresh chives
1 teaspoon chopped fresh chervil

Toss chicken in flour, shake away excess flour. Heat 2 tablespoons of the oil in pan, add chicken, cook until lightly browned. Transfer chicken to ovenproof dish (8 cup capacity). Heat remaining oil in same pan, add onion and garlic, cook, stirring, until onion is soft. Add tarragon, vinegar and wine, simmer, uncovered, until reduced by about one-third. Add broth and cream, simmer further 3 minutes. Pour sauce over chicken, bake, covered, in 350°F oven about 30 minutes or until chicken is cooked through. Serve chicken sprinkled with herbs.

Serves 4.

▪ Recipe can be made a day ahead.
▪ Storage: Covered, in refrigerator.
▪ Freeze: Not suitable.
▪ Microwave: Not suitable.

CURRIED CHICKEN CASSEROLE

2½lb chicken thighs, boned, skinned
1 teaspoon chili flakes
1 teaspoon ground cumin
1 teaspoon ground coriander
1 teaspoon garam masala
¼ teaspoon ground cardamom
½ teaspoon ground gingerroot
2 teaspoons curry powder
2 teaspoons seeded mustard
4 teaspoons vegetable oil
4 teaspoons Oriental sesame oil

SAUCE
2 tablespoons butter
2 tablespoons all-purpose flour
1 cup chicken broth
¼ cup dry sherry

SAFFRON RICE
1½ cups (10oz) basmati rice
1 teaspoon Oriental sesame oil
1 medium onion, chopped
½ cup roasted unsalted cashews
2 teaspoons black mustard seeds
⅓ cup dried currants
⅛ teaspoon ground saffron
½ teaspoon paprika

Cut chicken thighs into 4 pieces. Combine chicken with spices in bowl; mix well. Heat oils in large skillet, add chicken mixture, cook until browned and cooked through. Pour sauce over chicken, stir until heated through. Serve with saffron rice.
Sauce: Melt butter in pan, stir in flour, stir over heat until dry and grainy. Remove pan from heat, gradually stir in chicken broth and sherry, stir mixture over heat until sauce boils and thickens.

Saffron Rice: Add rice to pan of boiling water, boil, uncovered, until tender; drain. Heat oil in pan, add onion, cook, stirring, until soft. Add rice, chopped cashews and remaining ingredients, stir over heat until rice is heated through.

Serves 4 to 6.

- Curried chicken casserole can be made a day ahead.
- Storage: Covered, in refrigerator.
- Freeze: Suitable.
- Microwave: Saffron rice suitable.

CHICKEN AND GARBANZO BEANS WITH COUSCOUS

2 tablespoons olive oil
3lb chicken pieces
2 medium onions, chopped
3 cloves garlic, minced
10oz can garbanzo beans, rinsed, drained
14½oz can tomatoes
3 medium zucchini, chopped
1 medium red bell pepper, chopped
1 small eggplant, chopped
⅛ teaspoon cayenne pepper
1 teaspoon paprika
1 teaspoon turmeric
1 bay leaf
2½ cups chicken broth
2 tablespoons cornstarch
½ cup water

COUSCOUS
4 cups water
1lb package couscous
2 tablespoons olive oil
3 tablespoons butter

Heat oil in pan, add chicken, cook until browned all over, drain on absorbent paper. Add onions and garlic to same pan, cook, stirring, until onions are soft. Return chicken to pan, add beans, undrained crushed tomatoes, zucchini, red bell pepper, eggplant, cayenne pepper, paprika, turmeric, bay leaf and broth, simmer, covered, 45 minutes.

Remove chicken from pan, stir in blended cornstarch and water, stir over heat until mixture boils and thickens. Return chicken to pan, stir until heated through. Serve with couscous.
Couscous: Heat water in pan, add couscous and oil. Stir over low heat about 5 minutes, or until couscous is tender, add butter; stir until melted.

Serves 6.

- Recipe can be made a day ahead.
- Storage: Covered, separately, in refrigerator.
- Freeze: Suitable.
- Microwave: Suitable.

LEFT: From left: Chicken with Tarragon Vinegar and Fresh Herbs, Curried Chicken Casserole.
BELOW: Chicken and Garbanzo Beans with Couscous.

SPICY CHICKEN WITH BANANA FRITTERS

2 tablespoons (¼ stick) butter
1 medium onion, sliced
2 teaspoons ground coriander
2 teaspoons garam masala
1 teaspoon ground gingerroot
4 boneless, skinless chicken breast halves
1 cup chicken broth
1 teaspoon cornstarch
½ cup sour cream

BANANA FRITTERS
4 medium bananas
all-purpose flour
1 egg, lightly beaten
4 teaspoons milk
½ cup packaged unseasoned bread crumbs
½ teaspoon garam masala
oil for deep-frying

Heat butter in pan, add onion, cook, stirring, until soft. Add spices, cook, stirring, 1 minute. Add chicken, cook until lightly browned all over. Stir in broth, simmer, covered, about 10 minutes or until chicken is cooked through. Remove chicken from pan; keep warm. Stir in blended cornstarch and sour cream, stir over heat until mixture boils and thickens slightly. Return chicken to pan, stir until chicken is coated in sauce. Serve chicken with banana fritters.

Banana Fritters: Toss bananas in flour, shake away excess flour. Dip into combined egg and milk, then combined bread

crumbs and garam masala; cover, refrigerate 20 minutes.

Deep-fry bananas in hot oil until lightly browned; drain on absorbent paper.

Serves 4.

- ■ Recipe can be prepared 2 hours ahead.
- ■ Storage: Covered, in refrigerator.
- ■ Freeze: Not suitable.
- ■ Microwave: Chicken suitable.

CHICKEN IN RED WINE WITH MUSHROOMS

2 tablespoons (¼ stick) butter
3lb chicken pieces
5 slices bacon, chopped
12 (about 10oz) pearl onions
2 cloves garlic, minced
1½ cups dry red wine
2½ cups chicken broth
¼ cup brandy
2 tablespoons tomato paste
1 bay leaf
2 sprigs fresh thyme
½lb button mushrooms
2 tablespoons all-purpose flour
2 tablespoons water

Heat butter in pan, add chicken, cook until browned all over; drain on absorbent paper. Add bacon, onions and garlic to same pan, cook, stirring, until onions are browned and bacon is crisp. Stir in wine, broth, brandy, paste, bay leaf and thyme.

Return chicken to pan, simmer, covered, 30 minutes. Add mushrooms, simmer, uncovered, further 10 minutes. Remove chicken from pan, stir in blended flour and water, stir over heat until mixture boils and thickens. Return chicken to pan, stir until heated through.

Serves 6.

- ■ Recipe can be made a day ahead.
- ■ Storage: Covered, in refrigerator.
- ■ Freeze: Suitable.
- ■ Microwave: Not suitable.

CREAMY CHICKEN PIE

3 cups all-purpose flour
8oz package cream cheese, chopped
½ cup (1 stick) butter, chopped
2 egg yolks
¼ cup water, approximately
1 egg yolk, extra
1 teaspoon milk

FILLING
4 teaspoons olive oil
2 medium onions, chopped
4 slices bacon, chopped
2 cloves garlic, minced
2½lb chicken thighs, boned, skinned, chopped
¼ cup (½) stick butter
¼ cup all-purpose flour
2 cups milk
1 cup (¼lb) grated cheddar cheese
½ cup grated Parmesan cheese
4 teaspoons seeded mustard

Lightly grease 11 inch pie dish. Sift flour into bowl, rub in cheese and butter; add egg yolks and enough water to make ingredients cling together. Knead gently on floured surface until smooth, cover, refrigerate 30 minutes.

Divide dough in half, roll one half until large enough to line base and side of prepared dish; trim edge. Cover pastry with paper, fill with dried beans or rice, bake in 375°F oven 20 minutes. Remove paper and beans, bake further 5 minutes or until lightly browned; cool.

Spoon filling into pastry case, brush edge of pastry case with combined extra egg yolk and milk. Roll remaining dough until large enough to fit top of pie, cover filling with pastry. Press edges together firmly, trim edges. Brush pastry with egg mixture, decorate with pastry leaves, if desired. Cut 4 slits in pastry, bake in 375°F oven about 35 minutes or until browned and heated through.

Filling: Heat oil in skillet, add onions, bacon and garlic, cook, stirring, until onions are soft; remove onion mixture from skillet. Reheat skillet, cook chicken in batches until browned all over.

Melt butter in clean pan, stir in flour, stir over heat until bubbling. Remove from heat, gradually stir in milk, stir over heat until mixture boils and thickens; stir in cheeses and mustard. Combine onion mixture, chicken and cheese sauce mixture in bowl, mix well; cool.

Serves 8.

- ■ Recipe can be made a day ahead.
- ■ Storage: Covered, in refrigerator.
- ■ Freeze: Suitable.
- ■ Microwave: Not suitable.

LEFT: Clockwise from left: Creamy Chicken Pie, Chicken in Red Wine with Mushrooms, Spicy Chicken with Banana Fritters.

DUCK WITH MADEIRA, BACON AND OLIVES

3½lb duck
2 tablespoons (¼ stick) butter
12 (about 10oz) pearl onions
1 bunch (about 20) small carrots
10oz button mushrooms
4 teaspoons madeira
4 teaspoons all-purpose flour
2 tablespoons water
2 tablespoons chopped fresh parsley

BACON OLIVE SEASONING
2 tablespoons (¼ stick) butter
1 medium (about ¾lb) leek, sliced
2 cloves garlic, minced
3 slices bacon, chopped
5oz button mushrooms, chopped
⅔ cup black olives, chopped
⅓ cup pine nuts, toasted
2 tablespoons brandy
2 teaspoons chopped fresh thyme
1 cup (2½oz) fresh bread crumbs

Remove neck from duck, cut off wing tips at second joint. Cut through skin of duck along center back. Using tip of knife, separate flesh from backbone on 1 side of duck, cutting through thigh joint, then, following the shape of the bones, gradually ease flesh away from bone. Holding rib cage away from duck, carefully cut the breast flesh away from the bone, cutting through wing joint.

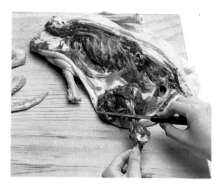

Hold up 1 thigh with 1 hand. To remove flesh, cut around top of bone, scrape down bone to next joint, cut around flesh again, scrape down to the end. Pull bone out and cut away. Repeat boning process with other half of duck. Turn flesh of thighs and wings inside duck.

Place duck skin-side-down on board, spoon seasoning along center of duck. Loosely roll duck to enclose filling, secure with toothpicks, tucking ends in neatly. Cover roll, refrigerate overnight.

Heat butter in skillet, add duck, cook until browned all over, transfer duck to roasting pan. Add onions and carrots to skillet, cook, stirring, until browned, remove from skillet; reserve onion mixture. Cover duck, bake in 325°F oven 1½ hours. Add reserved onion mixture and mushrooms to roasting pan, bake, uncovered, further 30 minutes or until duck is cooked through.

Remove duck and vegetables from dish; keep warm. Strain liquid from dish, skim away fat, add enough water to dish to make 1 cup of liquid. Place liquid in pan, add madeira, blended flour and water and parsley, stir over heat until sauce boils and thickens. Serve sauce with duck and vegetable mixture.

Bacon Olive Seasoning: Heat butter in pan, add leek, garlic and bacon, cook, stirring, until leek is soft, remove from heat, add remaining ingredients; mix well.

Serves 4 to 6.

- Recipe best prepared a day ahead.
- Storage: Covered, in refrigerator.
- Freeze: Not suitable.
- Microwave: Bacon olive seasoning suitable.

RIGHT: Duck with Madeira, Bacon and Olives.

APRICOT, GINGERROOT AND CHICKEN CASSEROLE

1 cup (5oz) dried apricots
2 tablespoons vegetable oil
4 boneless, skinless chicken
    breast halves
1 medium onion, sliced
3 cloves garlic, minced
2 tablespoons grated fresh gingerroot
2 teaspoons grated lemon zest
2 tablespoons chopped
    fresh thyme
¼ cup fresh lemon juice
½ cup apricot juice
2 tablespoons brandy
1 cup chicken broth
4 teaspoons cornstarch
2 tablespoons water

Cover apricots with boiling water in bowl, stand about 1 hour or until apricots are soft; drain.

Heat oil in pan, add chicken, cook until lightly browned all over; transfer to ovenproof dish (8 cup capacity). Add onion, garlic, gingerroot and zest to same pan, cook, stirring, until onion is soft. Stir in thyme, juices, brandy, broth and blended cornstarch and water, stir over heat until mixture boils and thickens. Pour broth mixture over chicken, stir in apricots. Bake, covered, in 350°F oven about 20 minutes or until chicken is cooked through.

Serves 4.

- Recipe can be made a day ahead.
- Storage: Covered, in refrigerator.
- Freeze: Suitable.
- Microwave: Suitable.

BELOW: From left: Fricassee of Chicken with Baby Vegetables, Apricot, Gingerroot and Chicken Casserole.

FRICASSEE OF CHICKEN WITH BABY VEGETABLES

7oz sugar snap peas
3½lb chicken pieces
all-purpose flour
¼ cup (½ stick) butter
2 tablespoons olive oil
1 medium onion, chopped
1½ cups dry white wine
4 sprigs fresh thyme
½ bunch (about 10) baby carrots
1 bunch (about 12) baby white turnips
7oz small button mushrooms
2 cups heavy cream
2 tablespoons all-purpose flour, extra
⅔ cup water
2 teaspoons chopped fresh thyme

Boil, steam or microwave peas until just tender. Toss chicken in flour, shake away excess flour. Heat butter and oil in skillet, add chicken, cook until lightly browned all over; drain on absorbent paper. Transfer chicken to clean pan, add onion, wine and thyme sprigs, simmer, covered, about 10 minutes or until chicken is cooked through. Add carrots, turnips, mushrooms and cream, simmer, uncovered, about 10 minutes or until vegetables are just tender. Remove and discard thyme sprigs. Stir in blended extra flour and water, stir until mixture boils and thickens; stir in peas and chopped thyme, stir until heated through.

Serves 4 to 6.
- Recipe can be prepared 2 days ahead.
- Storage: Covered, in refrigerator.
- Freeze: Not suitable.
- Microwave: Suitable.

CHICKEN ROASTED WITH GARLIC

9 (about 1¼lb) garlic bulbs
3½lb chicken
¼ cup fresh lemon juice
¼ teaspoon ground black pepper
1 bay leaf
2 sprigs fresh thyme
½ cup olive oil

CRISPY BREAD
1 large French bread stick
3oz (¾ stick) butter, melted

Break garlic bulbs into cloves; do not peel. Tie legs of chicken together with kitchen string, tuck wings underneath.

Brush chicken with combined juice and pepper. Place bay leaf and thyme inside chicken. Place chicken breast-side-up in roasting pan; place garlic cloves around chicken. Pour oil over chicken and garlic.

Cover chicken with greased foil, bake in 350°F oven 30 minutes. Remove foil, stir garlic, bake further 1¼ hours or until chicken is tender and garlic is soft; stir garlic occasionally. Spread garlic onto crispy bread, serve with chicken.

Crispy Bread: Cut bread into slices, brush both sides with butter. Place bread on baking sheet. Bake in 375°F oven about 10 minutes or until lightly browned and crisp.

Serves 4 to 6.
- Crispy bread can be made several days ahead.
- Storage: Airtight container.
- Freeze: Bread suitable.
- Microwave: Not suitable.

BELOW: Chicken Roasted with Garlic.

CHICKEN AND SWEETBREADS IN CIDER

½lb sweetbreads
3lb chicken pieces
all-purpose flour
2 tablespoons vegetable oil
1 tablespoon butter
16 (about 14oz) pearl onions
½lb button mushrooms, halved
1 clove garlic, minced
¼ cup (½ stick) butter, extra
2 tablespoons all-purpose flour, extra
1½ cups dry alcoholic cider
1 cup chicken broth
2 tablespoons brandy
¼ teaspoon ground nutmeg
2 bay leaves
2 tablespoons chopped fresh parsley

Cover sweetbreads with cold water in bowl, cover, refrigerate 3 hours or overnight.

Drain sweetbreads, add to pan of boiling water, boil 1 minute; drain. Remove membrane from sweetbreads; cut sweetbreads into 1¼ inch pieces.

Toss chicken in flour, shake away excess flour. Heat oil and butter in pan, cook chicken in batches until browned all over; transfer chicken to large ovenproof dish. Add onions, mushrooms and garlic to pan, cook, stirring, 3 minutes, transfer mixture to ovenproof dish.

Heat extra butter in pan, add extra flour, cook, stirring, until mixture is bubbling. Remove pan from heat, gradually stir in cider, broth, brandy and nutmeg, stir over heat until sauce boils and thickens. Pour sauce over chicken mixture, add bay leaves, cover, bake in 350°F oven 1 hour. Add sweetbreads, cover, cook further 15 minutes or until chicken is cooked through. Discard bay leaves; sprinkle chicken and sweetbreads with parsley.

Serves 6.

- Recipe can be made 2 days ahead.
- Storage: Covered, in refrigerator.
- Freeze: Suitable.
- Microwave: Not suitable.

ROCK CORNISH HENS WITH HONEY ORANGE GLAZE

¼ cup honey
¾ cup fresh orange juice
1 teaspoon horseradish cream
4 teaspoons finely chopped fresh lemon grass
1 teaspoon grated fresh gingerroot
3 tablespoons butter, melted
4 x 1lb Rock Cornish hens

HONEY ORANGE GLAZE
1 orange
2 teaspoons honey
½ cup fresh orange juice
1 teaspoon cornstarch
⅓ cup chicken broth
3 green onions, chopped
½ teaspoon horseradish cream

Combine honey, juice, horseradish cream, lemon grass, gingerroot and butter in bowl. Place hens in shallow dish, tuck wings under bodies, tie legs together. Pour over honey marinade mixture, cover, refrigerate several hours or overnight.

Remove hens from marinade, reserve marinade. Place hens on wire rack in roasting pan, brush with reserved marinade. Bake in 375°F oven 15 minutes; cover with foil if hens are over-browning. Reduce heat to 350°F, bake further 30 minutes or until cooked through, basting frequently with reserved marinade. Serve hens with hot honey orange glaze.

Honey Orange Glaze: Using vegetable peeler, cut peel thinly from orange, cut into thin strips; reserve 2 teaspoons peel strips. Combine reserved peel, honey, juice, blended cornstarch and broth, onions and horseradish cream in pan, stir over heat until glaze boils and thickens.

Serves 4.

- Recipe can be prepared a day ahead.
- Storage: Covered, in refrigerator.
- Freeze: Marinated hens suitable.
- Microwave: Not suitable.

RIGHT: From back: Chicken and Sweetbreads in Cider; Rock Cornish Hens with Honey Orange Glaze.

Beef

Old-fashioned country goodness is in every bite of these robust treats, yet they are often overlooked. They're not difficult to cook, either, whether it's beef Wellington for a smart dinner party, roast beef or corned beef for Sunday dinner, or simple Cornish pasties for school or work lunches.

BEEF OLIVES

½lb ground pork and veal
2 tablespoons chopped fresh parsley
2 cloves garlic, minced
1½lb thin top sirloin steaks
4 teaspoons olive oil
14½oz can tomatoes
1 small beef bouillon cube
½ cup dry red wine
1 teaspoon sugar
1 teaspoon seasoned pepper
3 tablespoons cornstarch
¼ cup water

Combine pork and veal, parsley and garlic in bowl; mix well. Flatten steak to ¼ inch with mallet. Cut steak into 8 strips 3 inches x 6 inches. Spoon pork and veal mixture evenly into center of each strip, roll steak up firmly, secure with toothpicks.

Heat oil in pan, cook beef olives until browned all over; transfer to ovenproof dish (8 cup capacity). Add undrained crushed tomatoes, crumbled bouillon cube, wine, sugar and pepper to pan, bring to boil, pour over meat. Bake, covered, in 350°F oven 1 hour, stir in blended cornstarch and water, bake, covered, further 45 minutes or until meat is tender and sauce thickened.

Serves 4.
- Recipe can be made 2 days ahead.
- Storage: Covered, in refrigerator.
- Freeze: Suitable.
- Microwave: Suitable.

CORNISH PASTIES

10oz top sirloin steak
1 small turnip
1 small carrot
1 small onion
1 small potato
¼ cup chopped fresh parsley
1 egg, lightly beaten

PASTRY
3 cups all-purpose flour
¾ cup (1½ sticks) butter, chopped
½ cup water, approximately

Cut steak and vegetables into ¼ inch cubes. Combine steak, vegetables and parsley in bowl. Roll pastry on lightly floured surface until ⅛ inch thick. Cut pastry into 5 inch rounds, top each round with ¼ cup of steak mixture. Lightly brush edge of rounds with egg, fold edges into center, pinch edges together to seal. Place pasties on greased baking sheet, brush with remaining egg. Bake in 350°F oven about 25 minutes or until browned.
Pastry: Sift flour into bowl, rub in butter. Stir in enough water to make ingredients cling together. Press dough into ball, knead on floured surface until smooth, cover, refrigerate 30 minutes.

Makes about 12.
- Pasties can be made 2 days ahead.
- Storage: Covered, in refrigerator.
- Freeze: Cooked pasties suitable.
- Microwave: Not suitable.

RIGHT: From top: Cornish Pasties, Beef Olives.

CORNED BEEF WITH CREAMY ONION SAUCE

If beef is to be served cold, allow it to cool to room temperature in the second cooking water.

4lb piece fresh corned beef
1 medium onion, halved
6 black peppercorns
1 medium carrot, chopped
1 teaspoon dark brown sugar
2 tablespoons brown vinegar

CREAMY ONION SAUCE
¼ cup (½ stick) butter
1 large onion, chopped
2 tablespoons all-purpose flour
2 cups milk
3 tablespoons chopped fresh parsley

Place beef in large pan, cover with cold water, bring to boil, drain. Cover beef again with cold water, add onion, peppercorns, carrot, sugar and vinegar. Bring to boil, simmer, covered, 2 hours, skimming occasionally. Remove beef from pan, drain well; discard vegetables and peppercorns. Stand beef 5 minutes before slicing. Serve with creamy onion sauce.

Creamy Onion Sauce: Heat butter in pan, add onion, cook, stirring, until very soft. Stir in flour, cook until bubbling. Remove from heat, gradually stir in milk, stir over heat until sauce boils and thickens, stir in parsley.

Serves 6 to 8.

- Beef can be cooked a day ahead.
- Storage: Covered, in refrigerator.
- Freeze: Not suitable.
- Microwave: Sauce suitable.

CURRIED STEAK AND ONION PIE

1½lb boneless beef chuck
2 tablespoons olive oil
2 large onions, sliced
1 clove garlic, minced
3 tablespoons curry powder
14½oz can tomatoes
½ cup beef broth
3 tablespoons all-purpose flour
¼ cup water
1 egg, lightly beaten
1 sheet (10in x 10in) ready rolled
    puff pastry

PASTRY BASE
1 cup all-purpose flour
2 tablespoons (¼ stick) butter
1 egg yolk
2 tablespoons water, approximately

Cut steak into 1¼ inch cubes. Heat oil in pan, cook steak in batches until well browned, remove from pan. Add onions, garlic and curry powder to same pan, cook, stirring, until onions are soft. Return steak to pan, stir in undrained crushed tomatoes and broth, simmer, covered, about 1½ hours or until steak is tender. Stir in blended flour and water, stir over heat until mixture boils and thickens; cool. Cover meat mixture, refrigerate until cold.

Spoon mixture into pastry case, brush edge with egg, cover with pastry sheet; press edge firmly to seal, trim edge; pinch to form a frill. Use leftover pastry to decorate top of pie, if desired. Brush with egg, bake in 375°F oven about 30 minutes or until pastry is browned and filling is heated through.

Pastry Base: Sift flour into bowl, rub in butter, stir in egg yolk and enough water to mix to a soft dough. Press dough into ball, knead on floured surface until smooth, cover, refrigerate 30 minutes.

Roll pastry out on floured surface until large enough to line base and side of greased 9 inch pie dish. Lift pastry into dish gently, ease into side, trim edge. Place dish on baking sheet, line pastry with paper, fill with dried beans or rice. Bake in 375°F oven 10 minutes, remove paper and beans, bake further 10 minutes or until lightly browned; cool.

Serves 4 to 6.

■ Filling can be made a day ahead.
■ Storage: Covered, in refrigerator.
■ Freeze: Suitable.
■ Microwave: Not suitable.

CORNED BEEF FRITTATA

1 medium onion, grated
2 large (about 14oz) potatoes, grated
1lb sliced cooked corned beef,
    finely chopped
4 eggs, lightly beaten
¼ cup chopped fresh parsley
2 tablespoons (¼ stick) butter
2 teaspoons olive oil
2 large (about 1lb) tomatoes,
    thickly sliced

Pat onion and potatoes dry with absorbent paper. Combine onion, potatoes, beef, eggs and parsley in bowl; mix well.

Heat butter in 12 inch omelet pan, swirl to coat base and side evenly. Add corned beef mixture, press mixture evenly into pan, cook over low heat about 30 minutes or until underneath is well browned and mixture firm. Place pan under heated broiler, broil until top is set and browned. Heat oil in large skillet, add tomatoes, cook until browned on both sides. Serve tomatoes with frittata.

Serves 4 to 6.

■ Recipe best made just before serving.
■ Freeze: Not suitable.
■ Microwave: Tomatoes suitable.

LEFT: From left: Curried Steak and Onion Pie, Corned Beef with Creamy Onion Sauce.
ABOVE: Corned Beef Frittata.

BEEF WELLINGTON

2lb piece beef tenderloin
3 tablespoons vegetable oil
7oz paté
¾lb piece frozen puff pastry, thawed
1 egg, lightly beaten

MUSHROOM FILLING
2 tablespoons (¼ stick) butter
1 small onion, finely chopped
14oz mushrooms, finely chopped
3 tablespoons dry white wine
2 teaspoons all-purpose flour

SAUCE
2 tablespoons all-purpose flour
½ cup dry red wine
1 cup beef broth
4 teaspoons Worcestershire sauce

Tie beef with kitchen string at 1¼ inch intervals. Heat oil in skillet, add beef, cook until well browned all over; cool. Remove string from beef. Reserve 2 tablespoons juices from skillet for sauce. Spread paté evenly all over beef, then spread with mushroom filling.

Roll pastry on floured surface to a rectangle large enough to enclose beef. Lightly brush edges of pastry with egg. Wrap pastry around beef, press edges to seal, place seam-side-down on greased baking sheet, decorate with pastry leaves, if desired; brush with remaining egg. Bake in 400˚F oven 10 minutes, reduce heat to 350˚F, bake further 30 minutes or until beef is cooked as desired. Serve beef Wellington sliced with sauce.

Mushroom Filling: Heat butter in skillet, add onion, cook, stirring, until soft. Add mushrooms and wine, cook, stirring, until mushrooms are soft and liquid is evaporated. Add flour, cook, stirring, until mixture is thickened; cool.

Sauce: Heat reserved pan juices in pan, add flour, stir over heat until browned. Remove from heat, gradually stir in wine, broth and sauce. Stir over heat until sauce boils and thickens; strain.

Serves 6.

- Recipe can be prepared a day ahead.
- Storage: Covered, in refrigerator.
- Freeze: Not suitable.
- Microwave: Not suitable.

SPICY SAUSAGES WITH OLIVES AND EGGPLANT

1 tablespoon butter
12 (about 10oz) pearl onions
8 (about 2lb) spicy beef sausages
3 cloves garlic, minced
15oz can tomato puree
½ cup dry white wine
½ cup black olives, halved
3 medium tomatoes, peeled, chopped
1 teaspoon sugar
1 medium (about 10oz) eggplant
½ cup olive oil
½ cup grated Parmesan cheese
¼ cup chopped fresh parsley

Heat butter in pan, add onions, cook, stirring, until lightly browned, remove from pan. Add sausages to same pan, cook until browned. Add garlic, puree and wine, bring to boil, stir in onions, olives, tomatoes and sugar, simmer, uncovered, about 10 minutes or until sausages are tender and sauce is thickened.

Meanwhile, cut eggplant into ½ inch slices. Heat oil in a large skillet, add eggplant, cook, turning once, until browned; drain on absorbent paper. Serve eggplant slices topped with the sausage mixture, cheese and parsley.

Serves 4.

- Recipe can be made a day ahead.
- Storage: Covered, in refrigerator.
- Freeze: Sausage mixture suitable.
- Microwave: Not suitable.

COTTAGE PIE

3 tablespoons butter
2 medium onions, chopped
2 cloves garlic, minced
1lb lean ground beef
2 medium carrots, sliced
¼ cup tomato paste
2 tablespoons chopped fresh parsley
1 cup beef broth
1 teaspoon celery salt

TOPPING
4 large (about 1½lb) potatoes
3 tablespoons butter
½ cup finely grated Swiss cheese

Heat butter in pan, add onions, garlic and beef, cook, stirring, until beef is browned. Add carrots, paste, parsley, broth and salt, simmer, covered, about 20 minutes or until carrots are tender.

Spoon mixture into ovenproof dish (6 cup capacity), spread with topping, roughen topping with fork. Bake, uncovered, in 375°F oven until heated through and browned.

Topping: Boil, steam or microwave potatoes until tender; drain. Combine potatoes with butter in bowl, mash until smooth, stir in cheese; mix well.

Serves 6.

- Recipe can be prepared a day ahead.
- Storage: Covered, in refrigerator.
- Freeze: Suitable.
- Microwave: Potatoes suitable.

LEFT: Beef Wellington.
ABOVE: From top: Spicy Sausages with Olives and Eggplant, Cottage Pie.

OXTAIL STEW

4lb oxtail, chopped
all-purpose flour
⅓ cup olive oil
4 sprigs fresh thyme
2 bay leaves
1 sprig fresh rosemary
4 sprigs fresh parsley
3 tablespoons olive oil, extra

2 cloves garlic, minced
1 medium onion, chopped
1 medium carrot, sliced
1 stalk celery, sliced
7oz speck, chopped
1 cup dry red wine
3 cups beef broth
⅓ cup tomato paste

Toss oxtail in flour, shake away excess flour. Heat oil in pan, cook oxtail in batches until browned, transfer to ovenproof dish (12 cup capacity).

Tie herbs in muslin. Heat extra oil in same pan, add garlic, onion, carrot, celery and speck, cook, stirring, until vegetables are lightly browned. Add wine, simmer, uncovered, until reduced by half. Stir in herbs, broth and paste, pour over oxtail.

Bake, covered, in 325°F oven about 3½ hours or until tender; cool, discard herbs, cover, refrigerate. Skim fat from stew before reheating.

Serves 8.

■ Recipe best made a day ahead.
■ Storage: Covered, in refrigerator.
■ Freeze: Suitable.
■ Microwave: Not suitable.

BEEF, SWEET POTATO AND OREGANO PIE

1¼ cups all-purpose flour
3 tablespoons butter
¼ cup water, approximately
1 egg, lightly beaten
2 sheets (10in x 10in) ready rolled puff pastry

FILLING
2 medium (about 1½lb) sweet potatoes
2lb boneless beef chuck
¼ cup olive oil
2 medium onions, sliced
4 cloves garlic, minced
⅓ cup chopped fresh oregano
½ cup all-purpose flour
⅓ cup tomato paste
1 cup dry red wine
3 cups beef broth

Grease deep 9 inch flan pan. Sift flour into bowl, rub in butter. Add enough water to make ingredients cling together. Press dough into ball, knead on floured surface until smooth; cover, refrigerate dough for 30 minutes.

Roll dough on floured surface until large enough to line prepared pan. Lift pastry into pan, ease into side, trim edge. Line pastry with paper, fill with dried beans or rice. Bake in 375°F oven about 20 minutes, remove paper and beans, bake further 10 minutes or until browned, cool.

Spoon filling into pastry case, brush edge of pastry with egg. Cover filling with 1 sheet of puff pastry, press edges together firmly, trim edge, brush top of pie with egg. Cut remaining puff pastry into 16 x ¾ inch strips. Place strips across pie to form lattice, trim edges, brush with remaining egg. Bake in 350°F oven about 30 minutes or until pastry is browned and filling heated through.

Filling: Cut potatoes and steak into ¾ inch cubes. Place potato cubes on baking sheet, bake in 350°F oven about 30 minutes or until tender.

Heat oil in pan, cook steak in batches until well browned all over, remove from pan. Add onions, garlic and oregano to same pan, cook, stirring, until onions are soft. Add flour, cook, stirring, until flour is lightly browned. Remove pan from heat, gradually stir in paste, wine and broth, stir over heat until mixture boils and thickens. Return steak to pan, simmer, uncovered, about 1¼ hours or until steak is tender. Stir in potato; cool.

Serves 6.

■ Filling can be made a day ahead.
■ Storage: Covered, in refrigerator.
■ Freeze: Suitable.
■ Microwave: Not suitable.

CABBAGE ROLLS WITH TOMATO SAUCE

⅓ cup orzo pasta
13 savoy cabbage leaves
14oz lean ground beef
1 clove garlic, minced
5oz prosciutto, finely chopped
3 tablespoons chopped fresh parsley
4 teaspoons chopped fresh chives
1 teaspoon beef bouillon powder
½ cup grated Parmesan cheese
¾ cup dry white wine
¼ cup beef broth

TOMATO SAUCE
4 teaspoons olive oil
1 medium onion, chopped
2 cloves garlic, minced
⅔ cup tomato puree
14½oz can tomatoes

Add pasta to large pan of boiling water, simmer, uncovered, until just tender; drain. Add 12 of the cabbage leaves to large pan of boiling water, cook until just wilted, drain; rinse under cold water, pat dry with absorbent paper.

Combine pasta, beef, garlic, prosciutto, herbs, bouillon powder and cheese in bowl; mix well. Spoon ¼ cup of beef mixture onto thick part of each leaf, roll leaves around mixture to form parcels. Place remaining cabbage leaf in base of pan, place cabbage rolls seam-side-down in a single layer over leaf. Add wine and broth, simmer, covered, 30 minutes. Stand 10 minutes before serving. Serve with tomato sauce.

Tomato Sauce: Heat oil in pan, add onion and garlic, cook, stirring, until onion is soft. Stir in puree and undrained crushed tomatoes, simmer, uncovered, until mixture is thickened slightly.

Serves 4 to 6.

■ Recipe can be made a day ahead.
■ Storage: Covered, in refrigerator.
■ Freeze: Suitable.
■ Microwave: Suitable.

LEFT: Clockwise from back: Beef, Sweet Potato and Oregano Pie, Oxtail Stew, Cabbage Rolls with Tomato Sauce.

VEGETABLE BEEF STEW IN RED WINE

2lb boneless beef chuck
all-purpose flour
3 tablespoons olive oil
15 (about ¾lb) pearl onions
1½ cups dry red wine
½ cup beef broth
4 medium carrots, chopped
4 stalks celery, chopped
1lb package frozen green
    peas, thawed
2 tablespoons chopped fresh parsley

Cut steak into ¾ inch cubes. Toss steak in flour, shake away excess flour. Heat oil in pan, cook steak in batches until well browned; drain on absorbent paper. Add onions to pan, cook, stirring, until lightly browned, add wine and broth, cook, stirring, 1 minute. Return steak to pan, simmer, covered, 1 hour, stirring occasionally. Add carrots and celery, cover, cook, further 20 minutes. Add peas, cook until steak is tender. Serve vegetable beef stew sprinkled with parsley.

Serves 4.

▨ Recipe can be made a day ahead.
▨ Storage: Covered, in refrigerator.
▨ Freeze: Suitable.
▨ Microwave: Not suitable.

STEAK AND KIDNEY POTS WITH BISCUIT TOPPING

2½lb boneless beef chuck
7oz sheep's kidneys
3 tablespoons olive oil
1 medium onion, chopped
2 slices bacon, chopped
¼ cup all-purpose flour
2 tablespoons tomato paste
3 cups beef broth
7oz flat mushrooms, chopped
1 medium green bell pepper, chopped
1 egg, lightly beaten

BISCUIT TOPPING
1½ cups self-rising flour
⅛ teaspoon cayenne pepper
⅛ teaspoon ground saffron
3oz (¾ stick) butter, chopped
⅓ cup milk, approximately

Cut steak into 1¼ inch cubes. Remove fat and membrane from kidneys, cut kidneys in half. Heat oil in pan, cook steak and kidneys in batches until browned; drain on absorbent paper. Reserve 4 teaspoons of pan juices.

Heat reserved juices in pan, add onion and bacon, cook, stirring, until onion is soft. Add flour, stir until combined. Remove from heat, gradually stir in paste and broth, stir over heat until mixture boils and thickens. Add steak, kidneys, mushrooms and pepper, simmer, covered, about 2 hours or until steak is tender.

Spoon mixture into 4 ovenproof dishes (2 cup capacity). Arrange biscuit topping over steak and kidney mixture, brush with egg, bake, uncovered, in 400°F oven about 15 minutes or until biscuit topping is lightly browned and cooked through.

Biscuit Topping: Sift dry ingredients into bowl, rub in butter. Add enough milk to make ingredients cling together. Press dough into ball, knead on floured surface until smooth. Press dough until ¾ inch thick, cut into 1½ inch rounds.

Serves 4.

- Steak and kidney mixture can be made a day ahead.
- Storage: Covered, in refrigerator.
- Freeze: Steak and kidney mixture suitable.
- Microwave: Not suitable.

LEFT: From back: Vegetable Beef Stew in Red Wine, Steak and Kidney Pots with Biscuit Topping.
BELOW: Beef Vindaloo.

BEEF VINDALOO

2lb boneless top blade steaks
1 teaspoon black mustard seeds
1 teaspoon cuminseed
1 teaspoon ground coriander
2 teaspoons curry powder
1 teaspoon grated fresh gingerroot
2 cloves garlic, minced
4 teaspoons vindaloo paste
2 tablespoons brown vinegar
4 teaspoons vegetable oil
4 teaspoons vegetable oil, extra
2 medium onions, sliced
14½oz can tomatoes
15oz can tomato puree

Cut steak into 1¼ inch cubes. Heat both seeds in dry pan, stirring until they pop, taking care not to burn; cool. Combine seeds, steak, coriander, curry powder, gingerroot, garlic, paste, vinegar and oil in bowl, mix well; cover, refrigerate overnight.

Heat extra oil in pan, add onions, cook, stirring, until soft. Add steak mixture, cook, stirring, 10 minutes. Stir in undrained crushed tomatoes and puree, simmer, covered, about 50 minutes or until steak is tender.

Serves 4.

- Recipe best prepared a day ahead.
- Storage: Covered, in refrigerator.
- Freeze: Suitable.
- Microwave: Suitable.

ROAST BEEF AND YORKSHIRE PUDDINGS

2½lb boned rolled piece beef sirloin
2oz dripping, melted
2 tablespoons chopped fresh
    tarragon
2 teaspoons seeded mustard
2 cloves garlic, minced
2 tablespoons all-purpose flour
1½ cups beef broth
3 tablespoons dry red wine
4 teaspoons Worcestershire sauce

YORKSHIRE PUDDINGS
1 cup all-purpose flour
2 eggs, lightly beaten
½ cup milk
¼ cup water

Place beef on wire rack in roasting pan, brush all over with dripping; bake in 350°F oven 1 hour. Spread beef evenly with combined tarragon, mustard and garlic, bake further 15 minutes or until the beef is cooked as desired.

Remove beef from pan, keep warm. Reserve 3 tablespoons pan juices for Yorkshire puddings.

To make gravy, drain remainder of pan juices, reserving another 3 tablespoons juices in pan. Stir flour into pan, cook, stirring, until lightly browned. Remove from heat, gradually stir in broth, wine, sauce and any juices that come from beef while standing. Stir over heat until mixture boils and thickens; strain. Serve sliced beef with gravy and Yorkshire puddings.

Yorkshire Puddings: Sift flour into bowl, make well in center, gradually stir in combined eggs, milk and water; beat well for 2 minutes, stand 30 minutes.

Pour ½ teaspoon of reserved pan juices into each hole of 12 x ⅓ cup muffin tins. Place in 400°F oven about 5 minutes or until juices are bubbling. Spoon pudding mixture quickly into prepared tins, bake in 400°F oven about 10 minutes or until puddings are well risen and lightly browned. Serve immediately.

Serves 6.

Recipe best made just before serving.
Freeze: Not suitable.
Microwave: Not suitable.

STEAK AND MUSHROOM PUDDING

You will need to buy about 10oz fresh suet for this recipe.

3 cups self-rising flour
2 cups (5oz) finely grated suet
1 cup water, approximately

FILLING
¼ cup olive oil
1 medium onion, chopped
2 cloves garlic, minced
2lb boneless beef chuck, chopped
14oz button mushrooms, quartered
¾ cup beef broth
¼ cup tomato paste
3 tablespoons Worcestershire sauce
½ teaspoon sugar

Lightly grease 8 cup capacity pudding steamer. Sift flour into bowl, stir in suet and enough water to mix to a soft dough. Knead dough on floured surface until smooth. Roll two-thirds of pastry large enough to line prepared steamer. Spoon filling into pastry case, brush edge with water. Roll remaining pastry large enough to cover filling, press edge firmly to seal; trim edge.

Cover steamer with greased foil, secure with kitchen string or lid. Place steamer in large pan with enough boiling water to come halfway up side of steamer; boil, covered, 2½ hours. Stand 5 minutes before turning out.

Filling: Heat oil in pan, add onion and garlic, cook, stirring, until onion is soft; remove onion mixture from pan. Add steak to pan in batches, cook until well browned all over. Stir in onion mixture, mushrooms and remaining ingredients.

Serves 8.

Recipe can be made a day ahead.
Storage: Covered, in refrigerator.
Freeze: Suitable.
Microwave: Not suitable.

BELOW: *Roast Beef and Yorkshire Puddings.*
RIGHT: *From left: Steak and Mushroom Pudding, Beef Rolls in Leek and Mushroom Sauce.*

BEEF ROLLS IN LEEK AND MUSHROOM SAUCE

1½lb lean ground beef
2 cloves garlic, minced
½ teaspoon ground cumin
½ teaspoon turmeric
1 cup (2½oz) fresh bread crumbs
1 egg, lightly beaten
1 medium onion, grated
1 teaspoon beef bouillon powder
¼ cup pine nuts, toasted, chopped
4 teaspoons chopped fresh mint
all-purpose flour
3 tablespoons olive oil

LEEK AND MUSHROOM SAUCE
4 teaspoons olive oil
1 medium (about ¾lb) leek, chopped
1 clove garlic, minced
½lb flat mushrooms, chopped
1 cup dry red wine
3 large (about 1½lb) tomatoes, chopped
3 tablespoons tomato paste
1 cup beef broth

Combine beef, garlic, spices, bread crumbs, egg, onion, bouillon powder, nuts and mint in bowl; mix well. Roll 2 level tablespoons of mixture into rolls about 3 inches long. Toss rolls in flour, shake away excess flour. Heat oil in skillet, cook rolls in batches until well browned all over; drain on absorbent paper.

Transfer rolls to shallow ovenproof dish (6 cup capacity), top with leek and mushroom sauce. Bake, covered, in 350°F oven 20 minutes, uncover, bake further 20 minutes.

Leek and Mushroom Sauce: Heat oil in pan, add leek, garlic and mushrooms, cook, stirring, until leek is soft. Add wine, cook, stirring, until almost all liquid is evaporated. Add tomatoes, paste and broth, simmer, uncovered, about 10 minutes or until thickened slightly.

Serves 4 to 6.

- Beef rolls and leek and mushroom sauce can be prepared separately a day ahead.
- Storage: Covered, in refrigerator.
- Freeze: Uncooked rolls suitable.
- Microwave: Leek and mushroom sauce suitable.

Lamb

Ask your butcher to bone out lamb cuts for you, and to butterfly the meat (cut it to lie flat) as required. We've given minimum cooking times, but you can cook until lamb is done as desired. Test by inserting a skewer into thickest part of lamb; if juices are clear, it's done. Our times will give slightly pink lamb.

ROAST LAMB WITH WALNUT HERB CRUST

2 x 1lb lamb loin roasts

WALNUT HERB CRUST
1 cup (3½oz) walnuts
⅔ cup fresh bread crumbs
¼ cup (½ stick) butter, melted
4 teaspoons chopped fresh thyme
1 teaspoon seasoned pepper

Press nut mixture over each loin roast, place lamb crust-side-up on wire rack in roasting pan. Bake, uncovered, in 375°F oven 15 minutes, reduce heat to 350°F, bake further 20 minutes or until lamb is cooked as desired.

Walnut Herb Crust: Process nuts and bread crumbs until fine. Transfer mixture to bowl, stir in butter, thyme and pepper.

Serves 6.

- Recipe can be prepared a day ahead.
- Storage: Covered, in refrigerator.
- Freeze: Prepared lamb suitable.
- Microwave: Not suitable.

LAMB WITH RATATOUILLE AND EGGPLANT

2 medium (about 1¼lb) eggplants
¼ cup olive oil
12 Frenched lamb rib chops

RATATOUILLE
2 medium zucchini
2 tablespoons olive oil
2 medium onions, chopped
2 cloves garlic, minced
1 medium red bell pepper, chopped
**8 small yellow pattypan
    squash, quartered**
**2 medium tomatoes,
    peeled, chopped**
14½oz can tomatoes
3 tablespoons tomato paste
1 teaspoon sugar

Cut eggplants into ½ inch slices, place slices on baking sheet, brush with oil, broil on both sides until browned. Broil chops until browned and tender. Serve chops on eggplant, topped with ratatouille.

Ratatouille: Cut zucchini in half lengthways, slice. Heat oil in pan, add onions and garlic, cook, stirring, until onions are soft. Add zucchini, pepper, squash, chopped tomatoes, undrained crushed canned tomatoes, paste and sugar. Simmer, uncovered, until vegetables are tender and mixture is slightly thickened.

Serves 4 to 6.

- Ratatouille can be made a day ahead.
- Storage: Covered, in refrigerator.
- Freeze: Not suitable.
- Microwave: Ratatouille suitable.

RIGHT: From left: Lamb with Ratatouille and Eggplant, Roast Lamb with Walnut Herb Crust.

CASSOULET

1½ cups (11oz) haricot beans
2 bay leaves
3 sprigs fresh thyme
4 cloves
14oz piece of bacon
2 medium carrots, chopped
28oz can tomatoes
⅓ cup tomato paste
6 cups water
2lb shoulder of lamb, boned
4 garlic beef sausages
4 teaspoons olive oil
4 teaspoons olive oil, extra
2 cloves garlic, minced
1 medium onion, chopped

Place beans in bowl, cover with cold water, cover, stand overnight.

Tie bay leaves, thyme and cloves in piece of muslin. Drain beans, combine with bacon, carrots, undrained crushed tomatoes, paste and water in pan; add muslin bag, simmer, covered, about 1½ hours or until beans are tender.

Cut lamb into 1¼ inch cubes, cut sausages into thirds. Heat oil in skillet, cook lamb in batches until browned all over, remove from skillet. Add extra oil to same skillet, add garlic and onion, cook, stirring, until onion is soft. Add sausages, cook until browned all over. Add lamb and sausage mixture to bean mixture; remove and discard muslin bag. Remove bacon from mixture, remove rind, cut bacon into 6 pieces, return to pan. Simmer, covered,

further 30 minutes or until lamb is tender and sauce is thickened slightly.

Serves 6.

▪ Recipe can be made 4 days ahead.
▪ Storage: Covered, in refrigerator.
▪ Freeze: Suitable.
▪ Microwave: Not suitable.

BELOW: From left: Cassoulet, Racks of Lamb with Juniper Berries.
RIGHT: Lamb en Daube with Couscous.

RACKS OF LAMB WITH JUNIPER BERRIES

2 racks of lamb (6 chops each)
2 cloves garlic, sliced
2 teaspoons dried juniper berries
4 teaspoons fresh rosemary leaves
4 teaspoons vegetable oil
1 medium carrot, chopped
1 stalk celery, chopped
1 medium onion, chopped
1/2 cup dry white wine
1 cup water
3/4in sprig fresh rosemary
4 teaspoons all-purpose flour
4 teaspoons water, extra
1/2 teaspoon sugar
1 teaspoon light soy sauce
2 tablespoons chopped fresh parsley

Using sharp knife, make small incisions in lamb. Place a slice of garlic, a juniper berry and a few rosemary leaves into each incision.

Heat oil in flameproof dish, add carrot, celery and onion, cook, stirring, until onion is soft. Stir in wine, water and rosemary sprig. Place lamb over vegetable mixture. Bake, uncovered, in 375°F oven 20 minutes, reduce heat to 350°F, bake, uncovered, further 20 minutes or until lamb is tender.

Remove lamb from dish; keep warm. Drain juices, reserve 1 cup juices, discard pulp. Heat reserved juices in pan, stir in blended flour and extra water, sugar and sauce. Stir over heat until sauce boils and thickens slightly, simmer, uncovered, 5 minutes; stir in parsley. Serve sliced lamb with sauce.

Serves 4.

- Recipe best made just before serving.
- Freeze: Not suitable.
- Microwave: Not suitable.

LAMB EN DAUBE WITH COUSCOUS

1/4 cup (1/2 stick) butter
3 small (about 1 1/4lb) leeks, sliced
2 medium onions, sliced
3 cloves garlic, minced
3 tablespoons chopped fresh thyme
3 tablespoons chopped fresh parsley
3 tablespoons olive oil
3lb diced lamb
3/4 cup dry white wine
1/2 cup beef broth
1 teaspoon coriander seeds

PASTE
1/2 cup all-purpose flour
3 tablespoons water
4 teaspoons olive oil

COUSCOUS
2 1/4 cups boiling water
1lb couscous
3/4 cup (1 1/2 sticks) butter
2 cloves garlic, minced
2 teaspoons ground coriander
2 teaspoons coriander seeds
1/8 teaspoon ground saffron

Lightly grease ovenproof dish with lid (8 cup capacity). Heat butter in pan, add leeks, onions and garlic, cook, stirring, until onions are soft, stir in herbs; remove leek mixture from pan.

Heat oil in pan, cook lamb in batches until well browned; remove from pan. Add wine to same pan, stir until pan juices are well combined; stir in broth.

Place half the lamb into prepared dish, sprinkle with half the seeds, spread with half the leek mixture. Repeat layers, ending with leek layer. Pour over wine mixture. Seal lid by placing strips of paste around lid of ovenproof dish. Bake in 350°F oven 2 hours. Remove paste carefully from dish, serve lamb with couscous.

Paste: Sift flour into bowl, gradually stir in combined water and oil, mix to a soft dough. Knead dough on floured surface until smooth.

Couscous: Pour water over couscous in bowl, stand 3 minutes or until water is absorbed. Heat butter in pan, add garlic, ground coriander, seeds and saffron, cook, stirring, about 1 minute or until fragrant. Add couscous, stir until well coated and heated through.

Serves 6.

- Recipe can be made a day ahead.
- Storage: Covered, in refrigerator.
- Freeze: Not suitable.
- Microwave: Not suitable.

LAMB AND APRICOT HOT POT WITH BISCUIT TOPPING

4½lb shoulder of lamb, boned
3 tablespoons olive oil
2 medium onions, sliced
1 cup (5oz) dried apricots
2 cups beef broth
4 teaspoons all-purpose flour
3 tablespoons water
1 egg, lightly beaten
2 teaspoons sesame seeds

BISCUIT TOPPING
1 cup self-rising flour
2 tablespoons (¼ stick) butter
4 teaspoons chopped fresh chives
1 teaspoon chopped fresh thyme
3 tablespoons chopped fresh parsley
¼ cup milk, approximately

Cut lamb into 1¼ inch cubes. Heat oil in pan, add lamb in batches, cook until browned all over; remove from pan. Add onions to same pan, cook, stirring, until soft. Return lamb to pan, add apricots and broth, simmer, covered, about 1½ hours or until lamb is tender.

Stir blended flour and water into lamb mixture, stir over heat until mixture boils and thickens. Spoon mixture into deep ovenproof dish (5 cup capacity). Place biscuits over lamb mixture, brush with egg, sprinkle with seeds. Bake, uncovered, in 375°F oven about 20 minutes or until biscuits are well browned and cooked through.

Biscuit Topping: Sift flour into bowl, rub in butter, stir in herbs and enough milk to mix to a soft dough. Knead dough on lightly floured surface until smooth. Roll dough to ½ inch thickness; using a cutter, cut into 1½ inch rounds.

Serves 4 to 6.

- Recipe can be made a day ahead
- Storage: Covered, in refrigerator.
- Freeze: Suitable.
- Microwave: Not suitable.

LAMB CASSEROLE WITH RAISINS AND LEEKS

3lb shoulder of lamb, boned
2 tablespoons olive oil
2 stalks celery, chopped
2 small (about 14oz) leeks, chopped
1 medium onion, chopped
1 clove garlic, minced
½ cup dry white wine
¾ cup beef broth
1 teaspoon garlic salt
¾ cup dark seedless raisins
2 teaspoons chopped fresh thyme
4 teaspoons chopped fresh parsley
4 teaspoons chopped fresh oregano
⅔ cup sour cream

Cut lamb into 1¼ inch cubes. Heat oil in large pan, cook lamb in batches until well browned, remove from pan. Add celery, leeks, onion and garlic to same pan, cook, stirring, until onion is soft. Return lamb to pan, add wine, broth, salt, raisins and herbs, simmer, covered, about 50 minutes or until lamb is tender. Stir in cream, stir over heat, without boiling, until mixture is heated through.

Serves 4 to 6.

- Recipe can be made a day ahead.
- Storage: Covered, in refrigerator.
- Freeze: Not suitable.
- Microwave: Not suitable.

SPICY LAMB SAUSAGES WITH CURRY BUTTER SAUCE

6 spicy lamb sausages

CURRY BUTTER SAUCE
4 teaspoons vegetable oil
1 small onion, finely chopped
2 cloves garlic, minced
¼ teaspoon ground fennel
¼ teaspoon ground gingerroot
¼ teaspoon garam masala
¼ teaspoon ground coriander
1 teaspoon curry powder
1 teaspoon cumin
⅛ teaspoon chili powder
⅛ teaspoon paprika
⅛ teaspoon ground cardamom
½ small red bell pepper,
**   finely chopped**
1 teaspoon tomato paste
¼ cup (½ stick) butter, chopped
¼ cup fresh lemon juice
¾ cup heavy cream

MINTED CUCUMBERS
2 small green cucumbers,
**   peeled, chopped**
⅓ cup yogurt
2 tablespoons chopped fresh mint

Broil sausages until browned and cooked through. Serve sliced with curry butter sauce and minted cucumbers.

Curry Butter Sauce: Heat oil in pan, add onion, garlic and spices, cook, stirring, until onion is soft. Add pepper and paste, cook, stirring, until pepper is soft, cool. Blend or process onion mixture and butter until smooth. Combine juice and cream in pan, simmer, uncovered, until reduced by half; gradually stir in butter mixture, stir over heat until melted.

Minted Cucumbers: Combine all ingredients in bowl; mix well.

Serves 4.

- Minted cucumbers can be made a day ahead.
- Storage: Covered, in refrigerator.
- Freeze: Not suitable.
- Microwave: Not suitable.

LEFT: Clockwise from left: Lamb Casserole with Raisins and Leeks, Lamb and Apricot Hot Pot with Biscuit Topping, Spicy Lamb Sausages with Curry Butter Sauce.

LAMB, ARTICHOKE AND PUMPKIN CASSEROLE

4lb leg of lamb, boned
1 cup (¼lb) frozen broad beans
    (fava), thawed
5oz pumpkin squash
3 tablespoons olive oil
¼ teaspoon turmeric
1 medium onion, finely chopped
1 stalk celery, chopped
2 teaspoons all-purpose flour
1 cup dry white wine
1 cup beef broth
2 bay leaves
8 pearl onions
8 artichoke hearts, drained
3 tablespoons fresh lemon juice
¼ bunch (5oz) spinach, shredded

Cut lamb into 1¼ inch cubes. Boil, steam or microwave beans until tender, remove and discard outer skins. Cut squash into ¾ inch pieces.

Heat oil in pan, cook lamb in batches until browned, remove from pan. Reheat same pan, add turmeric, chopped onion and celery, cook, stirring, until onion is soft. Add flour, cook, stirring, until combined. Remove pan from heat, gradually stir in wine, broth and bay leaves, bring to boil, return lamb to pan, simmer, covered, 1 hour.

Add squash and pearl onions, simmer, uncovered, further 20 minutes or until lamb is tender, stirring occasionally. Add beans, artichokes, juice and spinach, stir until spinach is wilted and casserole is heated through.

Serves 4.

- Recipe can be made a day ahead.
- Storage: Covered, in refrigerator.
- Freeze: Not suitable.
- Microwave: Broad beans suitable.

BUTTERFLIED GARLIC LAMB WITH POTATOES

10 large (about 4lb) baking potatoes
2 tablespoons (¼ stick) butter
4 teaspoons olive oil
6 cloves garlic, minced
3 tablespoons chopped fresh thyme
3 tablespoons chopped fresh
    rosemary
2 teaspoons seasoned pepper
4 teaspoons olive oil, extra
4lb leg of lamb, butterflied

Peel potatoes, cut potatoes into 1¼ inch chunks. Heat butter and oil in roasting pan, add potatoes, turn to coat potatoes evenly with butter mixture.

Combine garlic, herbs, pepper and extra oil in bowl. Rub half the garlic mixture on cut side of lamb, place lamb over potatoes, fat-side-up. Rub remaining garlic mixture over fat side of lamb. Bake, uncovered, in 375°F oven about 50 minutes or until lamb is tender.

Remove lamb from pan, keep warm. Drain away excess juice from pan. Return potatoes to oven, bake in 450°F oven about 20 minutes or until browned and crisp. Serve sliced lamb with potatoes.

Serves 6.

- Recipe best made just before serving.
- Freeze: Not suitable.
- Microwave: Not suitable.

LEG OF LAMB WITH HARICOT BEANS

2 cups (14½oz) haricot beans
4lb leg of lamb
4 sprigs fresh rosemary
4 cloves garlic, sliced
¼ cup olive oil
¼ cup (½ stick) butter
1 clove garlic, minced
1 medium onion, chopped
2 slices bacon, chopped
4 green onions, chopped
2 teaspoons chopped fresh rosemary
28oz can tomatoes
3 tablespoons tomato paste
1 teaspoon sugar

Place beans in bowl, cover with cold water, cover, stand overnight; drain.

Cut 4 slits in top of lamb, insert rosemary sprigs and sliced garlic. Place lamb on wire rack in roasting pan, pour over oil. Bake, uncovered, in 375°F oven 15 minutes. Reduce heat to 350°F, bake further 1¾ hours or until lamb is cooked as desired.

Meanwhile, add beans to large pan of boiling water, simmer, uncovered, about 1 hour or until tender, drain.

Heat butter in pan, add minced garlic, onion, bacon and green onions, cook, stirring, until onion is soft. Stir in chopped rosemary, undrained crushed tomatoes, paste and sugar, simmer, uncovered, until thickened. Add beans, stir over heat until beans are heated through. Serve lamb with haricot beans.

Serves 6.

- Haricot beans can be cooked a day ahead.
- Storage: Covered, in refrigerator.
- Freeze: Not suitable.
- Microwave: Beans suitable.

LEFT: From left: Lamb, Artichoke and Pumpkin Casserole, Butterflied Garlic Lamb with Potatoes.
ABOVE: Leg of Lamb with Haricot Beans.

BRAISED LAMB SHANKS WITH CELERY

When in season you can substitute fennel for the celery in this recipe. You will need 3 small (about 1¼lb) fennel bulbs, cut into quarters.

1 bunch (about 8 stalks) celery
2 tablespoons olive oil
2 medium onions, chopped
3 cloves garlic, minced
2 medium carrots, thickly sliced
4 teaspoons olive oil, extra
6 (about 4lb) lamb shanks
½ cup dry white wine
3 tablespoons tomato paste
2 cups beef broth
3 tablespoons chopped fresh thyme

Cut celery into 1½ inch lengths. Heat oil in pan, add celery, onions, garlic and carrots, cook, stirring, until onions are soft; remove vegetables from pan.

Heat extra oil in pan, add shanks, cook until well browned all over. Stir in wine, paste, broth and thyme, simmer, covered, 1 hour. Return vegetables to pan, simmer, covered, about 30 minutes or until shanks are tender.

Serves 4 to 6.

- Recipe can be made a day ahead.
- Storage: Covered, in refrigerator.
- Freeze: Suitable.
- Microwave: Not suitable.

NAVARIN OF LAMB

4 teaspoons oil
2 tablespoons (¼ stick) butter
8 medium (about 2½lb) lamb neck slices
1 medium onion, chopped
2 cloves garlic, minced
3 tablespoons all-purpose flour
½ cup dry red wine
4 cups beef broth
3 tablespoons tomato paste
4 teaspoons fresh rosemary leaves
4 teaspoons chopped fresh thyme
8 small new potatoes
2 medium carrots, chopped
8 pearl onions

Heat oil and butter in pan, cook lamb in batches until well browned, transfer to ovenproof dish (12 cup capacity). Add onion and garlic to same pan, cook, stirring, until onion is soft. Add flour, stir until lightly browned. Remove from heat, gradually stir in wine, simmer, uncovered, 2 minutes, stir in broth, paste and herbs. Bring to boil, pour sauce over lamb. Add potatoes, carrots and pearl onions to dish. Bake, covered, in 350°F oven about 1½ hours or until lamb is tender.

Remove lamb and vegetables from pan. Boil sauce until slightly thickened, strain, serve sauce poured over lamb mixture.

Serves 8.

- Recipe can be made a day ahead.
- Storage: Covered, in refrigerator.
- Freeze: Suitable.
- Microwave: Not suitable.

LAMB WITH VINEGAR AND GREEN BEANS

1lb green beans
3lb shoulder of lamb, boned
4 teaspoons vegetable oil
3 tablespoons vegetable oil, extra
1 small leek, chopped
2 cloves garlic, minced
1 teaspoon beef bouillon powder
½ cup white wine vinegar

Cut beans into 1½ inch lengths. Cut lamb into 1¼ inch cubes.

Heat oil in pan, cook lamb in batches until browned; remove from pan. Heat extra oil in same pan, add leek and garlic, cook, stirring, until leek is soft. Return lamb to pan, add beans, bouillon powder and vinegar, simmer, covered, 40 minutes. Remove cover, simmer further 10 minutes or until lamb is tender and liquid is almost absorbed.

Serves 4.

- Recipe can be made a day ahead.
- Storage: Covered, in refrigerator.
- Freeze: Not suitable.
- Microwave: Suitable.

LEFT: From back: Navarin of Lamb, Braised Lamb Shanks with Celery. BELOW: Lamb with Vinegar and Green Beans.

GLAZED LAMB WITH SPINACH SEASONING

2¾lb shoulder of lamb, boned
4 teaspoons olive oil
1 clove garlic, minced
1 large baking potato, chopped
1 large parsnip, chopped
1 large onion, chopped
2 teaspoons grated fresh gingerroot
1 cup dry white wine
1 cup beef broth
4 teaspoons chutney
2 teaspoons all-purpose flour
½ cup heavy cream

SPINACH SEASONING
2 tablespoons (¼ stick) butter
½ teaspoon garam masala
½ teaspoon ground nutmeg
3½oz flat mushrooms, finely chopped
1 medium onion, finely chopped
10oz package frozen spinach, thawed
1 cup (2½oz) fresh bread crumbs
3 tablespoons chopped fresh basil
1 egg, lightly beaten

Spread spinach seasoning over lamb, roll up, secure with kitchen string at 1½ inch intervals. Rub lamb all over with oil and garlic. Place lamb, potato, parsnip and onion in large pan. Add gingerroot, wine and broth, simmer, covered, about 30 minutes or until lamb is tender, turning lamb occasionally.

Remove lamb from pan, transfer to roasting pan. Strain pan juices; reserve juices and vegetables separately. Combine 4 teaspoons pan juices with chutney, spread over lamb. Bake, uncovered, in 400°F oven about 15 minutes or until lamb is glazed and heated through. Reheat reserved juices in pan, stir in blended flour and cream, stir over heat until mixture boils and thickens; return vegetables to sauce. Serve lamb sliced with sauce.

Spinach Seasoning: Heat butter in pan, add spices, mushrooms and onion, cook, stirring, until onion is soft. Squeeze excess juice from spinach, add spinach to onion mixture; stir over heat until moisture is evaporated. Transfer mixture to bowl, stir in bread crumbs, basil and egg.

Serves 4.

- Recipe can be prepared a day ahead.
- Storage: Covered, in refrigerator.
- Freeze: Uncooked seasoned lamb suitable.
- Microwave: Not suitable.

MINT SEASONED SHOULDER OF LAMB

3 tablespoons butter
1 medium onion, chopped
1 clove garlic, minced
4 teaspoons grated fresh gingerroot
¼ cup chopped fresh mint
1 teaspoon grated lemon zest
4 cups (10oz) fresh bread crumbs
2 tablespoons (¼ stick) butter, melted, extra

3lb shoulder of lamb, boned
4 teaspoons all-purpose flour
¼ cup dry white wine
1 cup beef broth
4 teaspoons chopped fresh mint, extra

Heat butter in skillet, add onion, garlic and gingerroot, cook, stirring, until onion is soft. Combine onion mixture, mint, zest, bread crumbs and extra butter in bowl, mix well; cool. Spread mixture over inside of lamb, roll up, secure with kitchen string at 1½ inch intervals. Place lamb on wire rack in roasting pan, bake, uncovered, in 350°F oven about 40 minutes or until lamb is tender.

Remove lamb from dish, keep warm. Heat juices in dish, add flour, cook, stirring, until flour is lightly browned. Remove from heat, gradually stir in wine, broth and extra mint, stir over heat until sauce boils and thickens. Serve lamb with sauce.

Serves 4 to 6.

- Recipe can be prepared a day ahead.
- Storage: Covered, in refrigerator.
- Freeze: Uncooked seasoned lamb suitable.
- Microwave: Not suitable.

SHEPHERD'S PIE

4 teaspoons vegetable oil
1 medium onion, chopped
2lb lean ground lamb
1 large carrot, chopped
¼ cup tomato paste
4 teaspoons Worcestershire sauce
1 cup beef broth
1 teaspoon chopped fresh thyme
3 tablespoons chopped fresh parsley
1 teaspoon seasoned pepper
3 large (about 1¼lb) baking potatoes, chopped
¼ cup (½ stick) butter
1 egg yolk

Grease shallow ovenproof dish (6 cup capacity). Heat oil in pan, add onion and lamb, cook, stirring, until lamb is well browned. Add carrot, paste, sauce, broth, herbs and pepper, simmer, uncovered, about 15 minutes or until carrots are tender. Spoon mixture into prepared dish.

Boil, steam or microwave potatoes until tender; drain. Mash potatoes with butter and egg yolk until smooth. Spoon potato mixture into piping bag fitted with star tube, pipe potato over lamb mixture. Bake, uncovered, in 350°F oven about 20 minutes or until lightly browned and heated through.

Serves 6.

- Recipe can be made a day ahead.
- Storage: Covered, in refrigerator.
- Freeze: Suitable.
- Microwave: Potatoes suitable.

RIGHT: Clockwise from left: Glazed Lamb with Spinach Seasoning, Shepherd's Pie, Mint Seasoned Shoulder of Lamb.

LAMB PARCELS WITH MINTY PEA PUREE

6 double Frenched lamb rib chops
2 tablespoons (¼ stick) butter
3 sheets (10in x 10in) ready rolled
 puff pastry
1 egg, lightly beaten

MUSHROOM FILLING
2 tablespoons (¼ stick) butter
1 medium onion, finely chopped
3½oz mushrooms, finely chopped
2 teaspoons chopped fresh parsley
3 tablespoons chopped fresh rosemary
½ small red bell pepper,
 finely chopped

MINTY PEA PUREE
2 tablespoons (¼ stick) butter
1 medium onion, chopped
2 cups (½lb) frozen green
 peas, thawed
3 tablespoons chopped fresh mint
4 teaspoons sugar
3 tablespoons cider vinegar
1 cup water

Remove 1 bone from each double chop. Heat butter in skillet, cook chops in batches until well browned all over; drain on absorbent paper, cool.

Cut pastry sheets in half. Place chops on pastry sheets, top with mushroom filling, press on lightly. Brush edges of pastry with water, fold over pastry to enclose filling neatly, trim pastry to shape where necessary. Place parcels on greased baking sheets, brush with egg. Bake, uncovered, in 350°F oven about 25 minutes or until pastry is puffed and browned. Serve with minty pea puree.
Mushroom Filling: Heat butter in skillet, add onion, cook, stirring, until soft. Add mushrooms, herbs and pepper, cook, stirring, until pepper is soft; cool.
Minty Pea Puree: Heat butter in pan, add onion, cook, stirring, until soft. Add remaining ingredients, simmer, uncovered, until peas are soft. Blend or process mixture until smooth.

Serves 6.

- Recipe can be prepared a day ahead.
- Storage: Covered, in refrigerator
- Freeze: Uncooked lamb parcels suitable.
- Microwave: Mushroom filling and minty pea puree suitable.

CINNAMON LAMB CASSEROLE

3lb leg of lamb, boned
4 teaspoons vegetable oil
4 teaspoons butter
2 medium onions, finely chopped
1 clove garlic, minced
1 teaspoon grated fresh gingerroot
½ teaspoon ground coriander
½ teaspoon ground cumin
2 teaspoons chopped fresh rosemary
1 bay leaf
1 cinnamon stick

4 teaspoons light soy sauce
1 medium carrot, sliced
6 pearl onions
1 stalk celery, chopped
1 cup beef broth
4 teaspoons all-purpose flour
3 tablespoons water
3oz mushrooms, sliced
1 medium tomato, peeled, chopped

Cut lamb into 1¼ inch cubes. Heat oil in skillet, cook lamb in batches until browned all over. Transfer lamb to ovenproof dish (7 cup capacity). Heat butter in same skillet, add chopped onions, garlic and gingerroot, cook, stirring, until onions are soft, stir in spices and rosemary.

Spoon onion mixture over lamb, add bay leaf, cinnamon stick, sauce, carrot, pearl onions, celery and broth. Bake, covered, in 350°F oven about 1½ hours or until lamb is tender. Stir in blended flour and water, mushrooms and tomato, bake, covered, further 20 minutes or until mixture boils and thickens. Discard cinnamon stick and bay leaf.

Serves 6.

- Recipe can be made 2 days ahead.
- Storage: Covered, in refrigerator.
- Freeze: Suitable.
- Microwave: Not suitable.

LAMB SHANKS WITH TOMATO BASIL SAUCE

3 tablespoons olive oil
8 (about 6lb) lamb shanks
3 tablespoons butter
6 cloves garlic, sliced
¼ cup all-purpose flour
2 cups beef broth
½ cup dry red wine
15oz can tomato puree
1 bunch (16) green onion bulbs
1 cup shredded fresh basil
3 medium tomatoes, peeled, chopped

Heat oil in pan, cook shanks in batches until browned; transfer shanks to roasting pan. Heat butter in first pan, add garlic and flour, cook, stirring, until flour is lightly browned. Remove from heat, gradually stir in broth, wine and puree, simmer, uncovered, about 20 minutes or until sauce is slightly thickened. Pour sauce over shanks, bake, covered, in 325°F oven 1½ hours. Add trimmed onions, basil and tomatoes, bake, covered, further 20 minutes or until mixture boils.

Serves 4 to 6.

- Recipe can be made a day ahead.
- Storage: Covered, in refrigerator.
- Freeze: Suitable.
- Microwave: Not suitable.

LEFT: Clockwise from top left: Lamb Shanks with Tomato Basil Sauce, Cinnamon Lamb Casserole, Lamb Parcels with Minty Pea Puree.

Seafood

In this small but delectable variety of seafood is a tasty catch of ideas including baked fish, smoked fish, a fresh salmon tart and fish in pastry. Look out, too, for a special recipe using salt cod, available in Greek and Italian delicatessens. As an added bonus, several recipes can be adapted to barbequing methods with great results.

SALMON, CHERVIL AND BROCCOLI TART

1½ cups all-purpose flour
⅓ cup grated Parmesan cheese
3oz (¾ stick) butter, chopped
1 egg yolk
3 tablespoons water, approximately
½ cup water, extra
¼ cup dry white wine
1 bay leaf
2 (about 14oz) salmon fillets
5oz broccoli, chopped
¼ teaspoon paprika

FILLING
3 eggs, lightly beaten
1 cup sour cream
2 teaspoons chopped fresh chervil

Lightly grease 9 inch flan pan. Sift flour into bowl, stir in cheese, rub in butter, add egg yolk and enough water to make ingredients cling together. Knead dough on floured surface until smooth, cover, refrigerate 30 minutes.

Roll dough between sheets of baking paper until large enough to line prepared pan. Lift pastry into pan, ease into side, trim edge. Cover pastry with paper, fill with dried beans or rice, place pan on baking sheet. Bake in 375°F oven 12 minutes, remove paper and beans, bake further 5 minutes or until lightly browned; cool.

Heat extra water, wine and bay leaf in pan, add salmon, simmer, uncovered, about 5 minutes or until just tender; drain, cool. Remove skin from salmon, cut salmon into small pieces. Boil, steam or microwave broccoli until just tender; drain.

Pat broccoli dry with absorbent paper.

Place salmon and broccoli into pastry case, pour over filling, sprinkle with paprika. Bake in 350°F oven about 45 minutes or until firm.

Filling: Combine eggs, cream and chervil in bowl, mix well.

Serves 6.

- Recipe can be made a day ahead.
- Storage: Covered, in refrigerator.
- Freeze: Not suitable.
- Microwave: Broccoli suitable.

RIGHT: Salmon, Chervil and Broccoli Tart.

Transfer fish to serving plates; strain vegetable mixture, discard liquid. Serve fish topped with vegetable mixture.

Serves 4.

■ Recipe best made just before serving.
■ Freeze: Not suitable.
■ Microwave: Suitable.

LEFT: Seafood, Tomato and Dill Stew.
BELOW: From left: Salmon and Sorrel Pastry Parcels, Baked Fish with Zucchini and Tomato.

SEAFOOD, TOMATO AND DILL STEW

½lb cleaned squid
2lb boneless white fish fillets
2lb small mussels
¾ cup dry white wine
1 small onion, chopped
1 clove garlic, chopped
3 tablespoons vegetable oil
2 medium (about ¾lb) leeks, chopped
3 cloves garlic, minced, extra
½ cup dry white wine, extra
28oz can tomatoes
⅓ cup tomato paste
⅛ teaspoon ground saffron
3 tablespoons chopped fresh dill
1 teaspoon sugar
1lb uncooked shrimp, shelled

Cut squid into rings. Cut fish into 1½ inch pieces. Scrub mussels, remove beards. Heat wine, onion and garlic in large pan, add mussels, cook, covered, over high heat about 5 minutes or until mussels open; drain, reserve liquid.

Heat oil in large pan, add leeks and extra garlic, cook, stirring, until leeks are soft. Add reserved mussel liquid, extra wine, undrained crushed tomatoes, paste, saffron, dill and sugar, simmer, un-covered, 10 minutes. Add squid, fish and shrimp, simmer 5 minutes, add mussels, stir until seafood is tender.

Serves 8.

■ Recipe best made just before serving.
■ Freeze: Not suitable.
■ Microwave: Suitable.

BAKED FISH WITH ZUCCHINI AND TOMATO

8 sprigs fresh dill
2 x 1½lb white flesh whole fish
14½oz can tomatoes
¼ cup olive oil
1 red onion, chopped
¼ cup chopped fresh basil
2 teaspoons chopped fresh oregano
4 medium zucchini, sliced
½ teaspoon seasoned pepper
¼ cup fresh lemon juice

Place dill inside fish; score both sides of fish at 1¼ inch intervals. Place fish in roasting pan, pour over combined un-drained crushed tomatoes, oil, onion, herbs, zucchini, pepper and juice. Bake, uncovered, in 375°F oven about 40 minutes or until fish and vegetables are tender, brush with juices during cooking.

SALMON AND SORREL PASTRY PARCELS

4 salmon fillets
2 tablespoons (¼ stick) butter
8 sheets phyllo pastry
¼ cup (½ stick) butter, melted, extra
8 large sorrel leaves

TOMATO BASIL SAUCE
4 teaspoons olive oil
4 green onions, chopped
14½oz can tomatoes
½ cup fish broth
¼ cup dry red wine
1 teaspoon sugar
½ cup heavy cream
3 tablespoons shredded fresh basil

Remove skin from salmon. Heat butter in skillet, add salmon, cook quickly on both sides until lightly browned but not cooked through; drain on absorbent paper.

Layer 2 sheets of pastry together, brushing each with extra butter, fold pastry in half. Place 1 sorrel leaf on pastry, top with salmon, cover with another sorrel leaf. Fold pastry to form a parcel and enclose salmon, brush parcel with butter. Repeat with remaining pastry, butter, salmon and sorrel. Place parcels on greased baking sheet, bake, uncovered, in 400°F oven about 12 minutes or until browned. Serve with tomato basil sauce.

Tomato Basil Sauce: Heat oil in pan, add onions, cook, stirring, until soft. Stir in undrained crushed tomatoes, broth, wine and sugar, boil, uncovered, 2 minutes. Process mixture until smooth, push through fine sieve. Return mixture to pan, add cream, simmer, uncovered, until slightly thickened; stir in basil.

Serves 4.

- Recipe can be prepared 3 hours ahead.
- Storage: Covered, in refrigerator.
- Freeze: Not suitable.
- Microwave: Not suitable.

Clockwise from left: Baked Mullet with Oregano and Potatoes, Salt Cod Hash with Red Bell Pepper Mayonnaise, Anchovy Eggplant Slice.

ANCHOVY EGGPLANT SLICE

2 medium (about 1¼lb) eggplants
coarse (kosher) salt
¾ cup olive oil
2 medium red bell peppers
2 sheets (10in x 10in) ready rolled
   puff pastry
½ x 2oz can anchovy fillets,
   drained, chopped
6 green onions, chopped
2 teaspoons balsamic vinegar
4 teaspoons chopped fresh basil
2 teaspoons chopped fresh oregano
6 hard-boiled eggs, chopped
¼ cup pitted green olives, sliced
1 cup (2½oz) grated Parmesan
   cheese

Line deep 9 inch square baking pan with foil. Cut eggplants into ¼ inch slices, sprinkle with salt, stand 30 minutes. Rinse under cold water, drain, pat dry with absorbent paper. Heat oil in large skillet, cook eggplant in batches until browned; drain on absorbent paper.

Quarter peppers, remove seeds and membrane, broil peppers skin-side-up until skin blisters and blackens. Peel skin away, slice peppers thinly.

Place pastry sheets on ungreased baking sheets, bake in 400°F oven about 10 minutes or until puffed and browned. Trim to fit prepared pan.

Place 1 sheet of pastry, puffy-side-up, into prepared pan. Top with half the eggplant, then layers of peppers, anchovies, onions, vinegar, basil, oregano, eggs and olives; repeat layers, ending with olives. Top with remaining pastry sheet, puffy-side-down; press firmly, sprinkle with cheese. Bake, uncovered, in 350°F oven about 30 minutes or until hot.

Serves 4 to 6.

■ Recipe can be prepared a day ahead.
■ Storage: Covered, in refrigerator.
■ Freeze: Not suitable.
■ Microwave: Not suitable.

BAKED MULLET WITH OREGANO AND POTATOES

1 lemon
3 large (about 1¼lb) potatoes,
   thinly sliced
3 cloves garlic, minced
½ cup olive oil
3 tablespoons chopped fresh oregano
8 (about ¾lb) mullet fillets
3 tablespoons fresh lemon juice
3 tablespoons chopped fresh
   oregano, extra

Using a vegetable peeler, cut peel from lemon, cut peel into thin strips. Place potatoes, slightly overlapping, over base of roasting pan, pour over combined garlic, oil and oregano. Bake, uncovered, in 400°F oven about 20 minutes or until potatoes are just tender. Remove dish from oven, place fish skin-side-down on potatoes. Sprinkle with peel, juice and extra oregano. Bake, uncovered, in 400°F oven about 10 minutes or until fish is just cooked.

Serves 4.

■ Recipe best made just before serving.
■ Freeze: Not suitable.
■ Microwave: Not suitable.

SALT COD HASH WITH RED BELL PEPPER MAYONNAISE

1¼lb boneless salt cod
2 bay leaves
⅓ loaf rye bread
3 tablespoons olive oil
3 medium (about 1lb) potatoes,
   chopped
4 teaspoons olive oil, extra
½lb speck, chopped
3 tablespoons balsamic vinegar
few drops tabasco sauce
3 hard-boiled eggs, chopped
3 tablespoons chopped fresh chives
3 tablespoons chopped fresh parsley

RED BELL PEPPER MAYONNAISE
1 medium red bell pepper
2 egg yolks
½ teaspoon French mustard
2 teaspoons fresh lemon juice
1 cup light olive oil

Salt cod must be soaked in fresh water to remove excess salt and rehydrate the fish. Soak cod for 2 to 3 days in large bowl, covered, in refrigerator, change water frequently; drain.

Place cod and bay leaves in large pan of water, bring to boil, simmer, uncovered, about 10 minutes or until cod is tender, drain; discard bay leaves. Flake cod into pieces.

Cut bread into ½ inch cubes, place on baking sheet, brush with oil, bake in 350°F oven about 10 minutes or until crisp. Boil, steam or microwave potatoes until just tender; drain.

Heat extra oil in skillet, add speck, cook until well browned and crisp, drain on absorbent paper. Add potatoes to same skillet, cook, stirring, until well browned. Add cod, vinegar and sauce, cook, stirring, 2 minutes. Add bread cubes, speck, eggs and herbs, stir until heated through. Serve with red bell pepper mayonnaise.

Red Bell Pepper Mayonnaise: Quarter pepper, remove seeds and membrane. Broil pepper skin-side-up until skin blisters and blackens. Peel skin away, chop pepper. Blend or process yolks, mustard and juice until smooth. While motor is operating, gradually add oil in a thin stream, process until thick. Add pepper, process until smooth.

Serves 6.

■ Salt cod must be prepared at least
   2 days ahead.
■ Storage: Covered, in refrigerator.
■ Recipe best made just before serving.
■ Freeze: Not suitable.
■ Microwave: Potatoes suitable.

TUNA WITH BRAISED ONIONS

2 tablespoons (¼ stick) butter
3 tablespoons olive oil
8 medium (about 2½lb) onions, sliced
½ medium red bell pepper, sliced
½ medium green or yellow bell
    pepper, sliced
3 tablespoons balsamic vinegar
2 sprigs fresh thyme
4 tuna steaks

Heat butter and oil in skillet, add onions, cook, covered, over low heat about 45 minutes or until onions are very soft. Add peppers, cook, covered, further 10 minutes or until peppers are soft. Add vinegar, thyme and tuna, cook, covered, about 5 minutes or until tuna is just tender.

Serves 4.

■ Onions can be prepared a day ahead.
■ Storage: Covered, in refrigerator.
■ Freeze: Not suitable.
■ Microwave: Not suitable.

SMOKED HADDOCK WITH POTATO AND LEEK TOPPING

2lb smoked haddock
2 cups milk
2 bay leaves
¼ cup (½ stick) butter
⅓ cup all-purpose flour
3 cups milk, extra
¼ teaspoon ground nutmeg
⅓ cup grated cheddar cheese
⅛ teaspoon cayenne pepper
½ medium red bell pepper,
    finely chopped
4 teaspoons grated Parmesan cheese

POTATO AND LEEK TOPPING
2 tablespoons (¼ stick) butter
½ medium leek, chopped
3 large (about 1¼lb) potatoes,
    chopped
¼ cup sour cream

Combine haddock, milk and bay leaves in pan, simmer, covered, about 5 minutes or until haddock is tender. Drain, discard milk and bay leaves; rinse haddock well. Remove skin from haddock, flake haddock. Melt butter in pan, add flour, cook, stirring, until mixture is dry and grainy. Remove from heat, gradually stir in extra milk, stir over heat until sauce mixture boils and thickens.

Stir in haddock, nutmeg, cheese and cayenne pepper. Spoon haddock mixture into ovenproof dish (6 cup capacity), top with potato and leek topping, sprinkle with bell pepper and cheese. Bake, uncovered, in 375°F oven about 25 minutes or until browned and hot.

Potato and Leek Topping: Heat butter in skillet, add leek, cook, stirring, until leek is tender. Boil, steam or microwave potatoes until tender, drain; mash well. Stir in leek mixture and cream.

Serves 6.

■ Recipe can be made a day ahead.
■ Storage: Covered, in refrigerator.
■ Freeze: Not suitable.
■ Microwave: Smoked haddock, sauce and potatoes suitable.

LEFT: From back: Smoked Haddock with Potato and Leek Topping, Tuna with Braised Onions.
RIGHT: Octopus in Red Wine.

OCTOPUS IN RED WINE

1 medium eggplant
coarse (kosher) salt
4lb baby octopus
4 teaspoons olive oil
2 medium onions, chopped
3 tablespoons chopped fresh
    lemon grass
1 clove garlic, minced
½ cup dry red wine
1 cup tomato puree
½ cup water
4 teaspoons fresh lime juice
1 medium yellow bell pepper,
    chopped
1 medium green bell pepper, chopped
1 cup (7oz) orzo pasta

Cut eggplant into 1¼ inch cubes. Sprinkle with salt, stand for 20 minutes. Rinse eggplant under cold water, drain well, pat dry with absorbent paper.

Remove and discard heads and beaks from octopus. Heat oil in pan, add octopus, onions, lemon grass and garlic, cook, stirring, until octopus changes color. Add wine, puree, water and juice, simmer, uncovered, about 1 hour or until octopus is tender. Add peppers, cook about 10 minutes or until tender.

Add pasta to large pan of boiling water, boil, uncovered, until tender; drain. Serve octopus with pasta.

Serves 6.

▨ Recipe can be made a day ahead.
▨ Storage: Covered, in refrigerator.
▨ Freeze: Not suitable.
▨ Microwave: Pasta suitable.

Pork & Veal

Old-fashioned cuts such as pork neck and veal shanks make very good eating in our imaginative new dishes here. You'll easily recognize the delicious influence of European-style food throughout, plus there's a tasty homely brawn. For special times, a festive ham is decorated to simple perfection.

SAUSAGE AND SPINACH TAGLIATELLE

½lb pork sausages
3 tablespoons olive oil
2 medium (about 1½lb) leeks, chopped
3 cloves garlic, minced
1 medium red bell pepper, sliced
1 medium yellow bell pepper, sliced
1½ cups chicken broth
4 teaspoons seeded mustard
1 bunch (1¼lb) spinach, shredded
4 teaspoons cornstarch
4 teaspoons water
1lb spinach tagliatelle pasta

Broil or pan-fry sausages until cooked; drain on absorbent paper; cool.

Cut sausages into ½ inch slices. Heat oil in pan, add leeks and garlic, cook, stirring, until leeks are soft. Add peppers, broth, mustard and spinach. Cook, stirring, until spinach is just wilted. Stir in sausages and blended cornstarch and water, stir over heat until sauce mixture boils and thickens.

Meanwhile, add pasta to large pan of boiling water, simmer, uncovered, until just tender, drain. Serve sauce with pasta.

Serves 4.

■ Recipe best made just before serving.
■ Freeze: Not suitable.
■ Microwave: Pasta suitable.

ARTICHOKE, PANCETTA AND OLIVE PIZZA

2 packages (½ oz) active dry yeast
1 teaspoon sugar
1 teaspoon all-purpose flour
1 cup warm water
3 cups all-purpose flour, extra
⅓ cup olive oil
½ cup black olives, chopped
2oz can anchovies, drained, chopped
2 cloves garlic, minced
¼ cup olive oil, extra
2 medium onions, sliced
3 tablespoons chopped fresh basil
3 large (about 1½lb) tomatoes, sliced
3½oz sliced pancetta, sliced
12 artichoke hearts, quartered
5 cups (1lb) shredded mozzarella cheese

Lightly grease 2 x 12 inch round pizza pans. Combine yeast, sugar and the 1 teaspoon flour in bowl, stir in water; cover, stand in warm place about 10 minutes or until frothy.

Sift extra flour into bowl, stir in yeast mixture and oil, mix to a firm dough. Turn dough onto floured surface, knead about 10 minutes or until dough is smooth and elastic. Return dough to large greased bowl, cover, stand in warm place about 30 minutes or until dough is doubled in size.

Turn dough onto lightly floured surface, knead until smooth. Divide dough in half, roll each half large enough to fit prepared pans; stand, uncovered, in warm place about 20 minutes or until risen slightly.

Blend olives, anchovies, garlic and 3 tablespoons of extra oil until smooth. Heat remaining extra oil in skillet, add onions, cook, stirring, until soft; stir in basil. Spread olive mixture evenly over dough, top with tomatoes, onion mixture, pancetta and artichokes; sprinkle with cheese. Bake pizzas in 400˚F oven about 20 minutes or until well browned.

Serves 4 to 6.

■ Recipe best made just before serving.
■ Freeze: Uncooked pizzas suitable.
■ Microwave: Not suitable.

RIGHT: From back: Sausage and Spinach Tagliatelle, Artichoke, Pancetta and Olive Pizza.

VEAL AND MUSHROOMS IN CREAMY SAUCE

4 teaspoons olive oil
24 (about 1¼lb) pearl onions
4 teaspoons olive oil, extra
1½lb diced veal
4 cups chicken broth
2 medium carrots, chopped
1 bay leaf
7oz button mushrooms
1¼ cups heavy cream
¼ cup fresh lemon juice
4 egg yolks

CROUTONS
1 small French bread stick
¼ cup (½ stick) butter, melted

Heat oil in pan, add onions, cook until browned; drain on absorbent paper. Heat extra oil in pan, cook veal in batches until browned. Add broth, carrots and bay leaf, simmer, covered, 20 minutes. Add onions and mushrooms, simmer further 20 minutes or until veal is tender. Strain veal and vegetables from liquid, keep warm.

Return liquid to pan, boil, uncovered, until reduced by half. Remove pan from heat, gradually stir in cream, juice and egg yolks, stir over very low heat until heated through, do not boil. Return veal and vegetables to pan, stir until combined. Serve with croutons.

Croutons: Cut bread into ½ inch slices, brush both sides with butter. Place bread on baking sheet, bake in 350°F oven about 10 minutes or until lightly browned and crisp.

Serves 4.

▦ Recipe best made just before serving. Croutons can be made a day ahead.
▦ Storage: Airtight container.
▦ Freeze: Not suitable.
▦ Microwave: Not suitable.

BELOW: From left: Braised Veal with Polenta, Veal and Mushrooms in Creamy Sauce.

BRAISED VEAL WITH POLENTA

3 tablespoons olive oil
2½lb rolled veal roast
½ cup dry white wine
3 tablespoons butter
2 cloves garlic, minced
14oz button mushrooms, sliced
½ cup chicken broth
½ teaspoon French mustard
1 teaspoon cornstarch
2 teaspoons water

POLENTA
3½ cups water
1 cup (7oz) yellow cornmeal
2 teaspoons chicken bouillon powder
½ cup grated Parmesan cheese

Heat oil in pan, add veal, cook until browned all over. Add wine, simmer, covered, about 1 hour or until tender. Remove veal from pan, keep warm; remove and reserve pan juices.

Heat butter and garlic in pan, add mushrooms, cook, stirring, until mush-

rooms are soft. Stir in strained reserved pan juices, broth, mustard and blended cornstarch and water. Stir over heat until mixture boils and thickens slightly. Slice veal, serve with sauce and polenta.

Polenta: Bring water to boil in pan, add yellow cornmeal and bouillon powder, simmer, stirring, about 8 minutes or until thick and soft. Stir in cheese.

Serves 6.

- Recipe can be made a day ahead.
- Storage: Covered, in refrigerator.
- Freeze: Not suitable.
- Microwave: Not suitable.

PORK WITH WATER CHESTNUT SEASONING

4½lb boneless pork sirloin roast (rind attached)
4 teaspoons salt
4 teaspoons vegetable oil

WATER CHESTNUT SEASONING
⅓ cup wild rice
2 teaspoons butter
1 clove garlic, minced
1 stalk celery, chopped
3 green onions, chopped
1 teaspoon grated lemon zest
10oz can water chestnuts, drained, halved
2 teaspoons chopped fresh parsley
2 teaspoons chopped fresh tarragon
3 tablespoons grated Parmesan cheese
4 teaspoons packaged unseasoned bread crumbs

ORANGE GLAZE
1 medium orange
1⅓ cups fresh orange juice
⅓ cup brandy
2 teaspoons white vinegar
3 tablespoons honey
2 teaspoons cornstarch
4 teaspoons water
3 tablespoons chopped fresh tarragon

Place pork on bench, skin-side-up. Run knife ¼ inch under rind, gradually separating rind from meat. Place rind in roasting pan, sprinkle with salt. Bake in 450°F oven about 40 minutes or until rind browns and crackles; drain on absorbent paper; cool rind, cut into serving pieces.

Place pork on bench, fat-side-down. Horizontally slice through thickest part of meat (without cutting through to the side). Open out top piece to form 1 large piece of pork, press flat.

Spread water chestnut seasoning over pork, roll up firmly, secure with kitchen string at ¾ inch intervals. Place pork on wire rack in roasting pan, brush with oil; bake, uncovered, in 400°F oven about 1 hour or until pork is tender. Serve with crackling and orange glaze.

Water Chestnut Seasoning: Add rice to pan of boiling water, boil, uncovered, about 30 minutes or until tender; drain. Heat butter in pan, add garlic, celery, onions and zest, cook, stirring, until onions are soft. Remove from heat, stir in rice, water chestnuts, herbs, cheese and bread crumbs, mix well; cool.

Orange Glaze: Using a vegetable peeler, cut peel from orange, cut peel into thin strips. Combine juice, brandy, vinegar and honey in pan, stir in blended cornstarch and water, stir over heat until sauce boils and thickens; stir in peel and tarragon.

Serves 6.

- Water chestnut seasoning can be made a day ahead.
- Storage: Covered, in refrigerator.
- Freeze: Not suitable.
- Microwave: Rice and orange glaze suitable.

ABOVE: Pork with Water Chestnut Seasoning.

KNUCKLE OF VEAL WITH SUGAR SNAP PEAS

7oz sugar snap peas
3 tablespoons olive oil
3lb (about 6 pieces) veal knuckle
1 medium onion, chopped
1 stalk celery, chopped
2 sprigs fresh rosemary
2 sprigs fresh sage
3 tablespoons all-purpose flour
½ cup dry white wine
1 cup beef broth
½ cup tomato puree
7oz flat mushrooms, sliced
4 teaspoons Worcestershire sauce

Boil, steam or microwave peas until just tender, drain, rinse under cold water; pat dry with absorbent paper.

Heat oil in pan, add veal, cook until browned all over, drain on absorbent paper. Add onion, celery and herbs to pan, cook, covered, until onion is soft. Add flour, cook, stirring, until mixture is combined. Remove from heat, gradually stir in wine, stir over heat until mixture boils and thickens. Return veal to pan, add broth, puree, mushrooms and sauce, simmer, covered, about 1½ hours or until veal is tender. Add peas, stir until hot.

Serves 4.

- Recipe can be made a day ahead.
- Storage: Covered, in refrigerator.
- Freeze: Not suitable.
- Microwave: Peas suitable.

VEAL WITH APRICOTS AND MARSALA

3 tablespoons olive oil
3lb diced veal
1 medium onion, chopped
3 slices bacon, chopped
2 cloves garlic, minced
4 teaspoons tomato paste
2 cups chicken broth
½ cup chopped dried apricots
3 tablespoons marsala
½ cup heavy cream
¼ cup sliced almonds, toasted

Heat half the oil in pan, cook veal in batches until browned all over; remove veal from pan.

Heat remaining oil in same pan, add onion, bacon and garlic, cook, stirring, until onion is soft. Return veal to pan, add paste and broth, simmer, covered, about 1½ hours or until veal is tender. Stir in apricots, marsala and cream, stir until hot. Serve sprinkled with almonds.

Serves 6.

- Recipe can be prepared a day ahead.
- Storage: Covered, in refrigerator.
- Freeze: Not suitable.
- Microwave: Not suitable.

CRUSTY ROASTED SHOULDER OF VEAL

2½lb veal shoulder, butterflied
⅓ cup olive oil
1 large onion, chopped
3 tablespoons chopped fresh rosemary
½ cup dry white wine
½ cup beef broth
3 cloves garlic, minced
1 egg, lightly beaten
2 teaspoons seasoned pepper
¼ cup grated Parmesan cheese
¼ cup packaged unseasoned bread crumbs

GRAVY
4 teaspoons olive oil
2 tablespoons all-purpose flour
1 beef bouillon cube

Roll veal, tie with kitchen string at 1½ inch intervals. Heat oil in flameproof dish, add veal, cook until browned all over. Add onion, rosemary, wine, broth and garlic, bake, covered, in 375°F oven about 1¼ hours or until veal is tender.

Remove veal from dish; cool. Strain liquid from dish; reserve 1½ cups liquid for gravy. Refrigerate veal until cool.

Remove string from veal, dip veal in egg, roll in combined pepper, cheese and bread crumbs, press on firmly. Place veal on wire rack in roasting pan. Bake in 400°F oven about 20 minutes or until crust is browned and veal is heated through. Serve veal sliced with gravy.

Gravy: Heat oil in pan, add flour, cook, stirring, until browned. Remove from heat, gradually stir in crumbled bouillon cube and reserved liquid. Stir over heat until gravy boils and thickens.

Serves 4.

- Veal can be prepared a day ahead.
- Storage: Covered, in refrigerator.
- Freeze: Suitable.
- Microwave: Gravy suitable.

RIGHT: Clockwise from left: Crusty Roasted Shoulder of Veal, Veal with Apricots and Marsala, Knuckle of Veal with Sugar Snap Peas.

SMOKED PORK WITH MUSTARD CRUST

2lb piece kasseler (smoked pork)

MUSTARD CRUST
⅓ cup fresh bread crumbs
½ cup seeded mustard
½ teaspoon coriander seeds

TOMATO SAUCE
1 tablespoon butter
1 medium onion, finely chopped
1 clove garlic, minced
14½oz can tomatoes
½ cup water
1 teaspoon sugar
4 teaspoons chopped fresh basil

Using a sharp knife, remove rind from kasseler. Spread mustard crust over top of kasseler, refrigerate 10 minutes. Place kasseler on wire rack in roasting pan, bake, uncovered, in 350°F oven 45 minutes. Cover with foil, bake further 15 minutes. Serve with tomato sauce.
Mustard Crust: Combine all ingredients in bowl, mix to a paste.
Tomato Sauce: Heat butter in pan, add onion and garlic, cook, stirring, until onion is soft. Stir in undrained crushed tomatoes, water, sugar and basil. Simmer, uncovered, until slightly thickened. Blend or process sauce until pureed.

Serves 4.

■ Recipe can be prepared a day ahead.
■ Storage: Covered, in refrigerator.
■ Freeze: Not suitable.
■ Microwave: Tomato sauce suitable.

TASTY FARMHOUSE BRAWN

30oz veal knuckle, quartered
1lb boned beef shanks cross cut, chopped
2 medium onions, chopped
4 cloves garlic, minced
1 large carrot, chopped
1 teaspoon beef bouillon powder
6½ cups water
1 tablespoon gelatin
3 tablespoons water, extra

Line 5½ inch x 8½ inch loaf pan with foil. Combine veal, beef, onions, garlic, carrot, bouillon powder and water in pan, bring to boil, simmer, covered, about 2 hours or until meat is falling from bones.

Remove meat from bones, discard bones; chop meat roughly, return meat to pan. Sprinkle gelatin over extra water in cup, stand in pan of simmering water, stir until dissolved. Stir gelatin mixture into meat mixture, stir well. Pour mixture into prepared pan, cool. Cover pan, refrigerate overnight or until set. Turn out, serve brawn sliced.

Serves 6 to 8.

- Recipe best made a day ahead.
- Storage: Covered, in refrigerator.
- Freeze: Not suitable.
- Microwave: Gelatin suitable.

VEAL AND FENNEL CASSEROLE

¼ cup (½ stick) butter
3 cloves garlic, minced
1 teaspoon fennel seeds
2lb diced veal
½ cup all-purpose flour
1 cup dry white wine
¼ cup fresh lemon juice
4 cups water
½ fennel bulb, chopped
½ cup dry vermouth
⅓ cup sour cream
¼ cup chopped fresh fennel tips
1 egg yolk

Heat butter in pan, add garlic, seeds and veal, cook, stirring, until veal is browned all over. Add flour, cook, stirring, until combined. Remove from heat, gradually stir in wine, juice and water, stir over heat until mixture boils and thickens, simmer, covered, 1 hour. Stir in chopped fennel and vermouth, simmer, covered, 30 minutes or until veal is tender. Remove pan from heat, stir in combined sour cream, fennel tips and egg yolk.

Serves 4.

- Recipe can be prepared 2 days ahead.
- Storage: Covered, in refrigerator.
- Freeze: Not suitable.
- Microwave: Not suitable.

ROSEMARY VEAL CHOPS

2 slices bacon
4 veal rib chops
all-purpose flour
1 egg, lightly beaten
4 teaspoons milk
1½ cups (3½oz) fresh bread crumbs
4 teaspoons chopped fresh rosemary
1 teaspoon seasoned pepper
oil for shallow-frying
4 slices Swiss cheese

Cut bacon into thin strips. Trim fat from ends of chops, exposing the bones. Gently flatten veal using a meat mallet. Toss veal in flour; shake away excess flour. Dip veal into combined egg and milk, coat in combined bread crumbs, rosemary and pepper; refrigerate veal 30 minutes.

Shallow-fry veal in hot oil until tender; drain. Place veal on baking sheet, top with cheese and bacon, broil until cheese is melted and bacon is crisp.

Serves 4.

- Veal can be prepared a day ahead.
- Storage: Covered, in refrigerator.
- Freeze: Uncooked crumbed veal suitable.
- Microwave: Not suitable.

LEFT: From top: Smoked Pork with Mustard Crust, Tasty Farmhouse Brawn.
BELOW: From left: Veal and Fennel Casserole, Rosemary Veal Chops.

PORK WITH PRUNES AND CABBAGE

2lb lean piece pork neck
all-purpose flour
⅓ cup vegetable oil
1 medium onion, chopped
2 cloves garlic, minced
¼ cup brandy
3½ cups chicken broth
½ cup chopped pitted prunes
3 tablespoons chopped fresh oregano
4 teaspoons chopped fresh thyme
2½ cups (about 7oz) shredded
    cabbage

Cut pork into 1¼ inch cubes. Toss pork in flour, shake away excess flour. Heat oil in pan, cook pork in batches until browned. Transfer pork to ovenproof dish (12 cup capacity). Add onion and garlic to same pan, cook, stirring, until onion is soft. Add brandy, broth, prunes, oregano and thyme, simmer, uncovered, 3 minutes. Pour sauce over pork in dish, add cabbage, bake, covered, in 350°F oven about 1 hour or until pork is tender.

Serves 6.

▪ Recipe can be made a day ahead.
▪ Storage: Covered, in refrigerator.
▪ Freeze: Not suitable.
▪ Microwave: Not suitable.

LEEK AND HAM PIE WITH CUMBERLAND SAUCE

½lb sliced cooked ham
3 tablespoons butter
2 medium (about 1½lb) leeks, sliced
10 sheets phyllo pastry
3oz (¾ stick) butter, melted, extra
3 tablespoons packaged unseasoned
    bread crumbs
8oz container sour cream
3 tablespoons chopped fresh chives

CUMBERLAND SAUCE
1 medium lemon
2 medium oranges
3 tablespoons redcurrant jelly
¼ cup port wine
½ teaspoon French mustard
2 green onions, chopped

Lightly grease 9 inch pie plate. Cut ham into thin strips. Heat butter in pan, add leeks, cook, stirring, until soft; drain.

Brush a sheet of phyllo pastry with some of the extra butter, fold in half lengthways. Place pastry strip in pie plate, allowing pastry to overhang edge of pie plate. Repeat with remaining pastry and more extra butter, lining pie plate with pastry in a clockwise motion; see picture.

Sprinkle pastry case with bread crumbs. Place half the ham in pastry case, top with leeks. Spread combined sour cream and chives over leeks, top with remaining ham. Lift pastry edges towards center of pie to encase filling,

pinch pastry together in center, brush pastry with remaining extra butter. Bake pie in 350°F oven 30 minutes. Cover pie with foil if over-browning. Serve pie with Cumberland sauce.

Cumberland Sauce: Cut peel thinly from lemon and 1 of the oranges. Cut peel into thin strips. Place peel in pan, cover with water, boil, uncovered, 3 minutes; drain. Squeeze juice from lemon and both oranges; you will need 3 tablespoons lemon juice and ½ cup orange juice. Combine peel, juices, jelly, port wine and mustard in pan, bring to boil, simmer, uncovered, 2 minutes, stir in onions; cool.

Serves 6.

▪ Pie and sauce can be made
    a day ahead.
▪ Storage: Covered, in refrigerator.
▪ Freeze: Not suitable.
▪ Microwave: Sauce suitable.

GLAZED HAM WITH TAMARILLO SAUCE

1 small (about 13lb) leg of ham
1 small fresh pineapple, thinly sliced

GLAZE
½ cup apricot jam
¼ cup papaya and mango chutney
3 tablespoons brandy
⅓ cup water
2 teaspoons Worcestershire sauce

TAMARILLO SAUCE
10 (about 30oz) tamarillos
½ cup dark brown sugar
⅓ cup water
6 green onions, chopped
1 cup chicken broth
½ cup dry white wine
4 teaspoons cornstarch
3 tablespoons water, extra

Cut through rind of ham about 6 inches from shank end in decorative pattern. To remove rind from ham, run thumb around edge of rind just under skin. Start pulling rind from widest edge of ham, continue to pull the rind carefully away from fat up to the decorative pattern.

Make shallow cuts in the fat diagonally at 1¼ inch intervals. Brush with half the glaze, bake in 350°F oven 30 minutes. Cut pineapple slices in half crossways, overlap on ham, securing with toothpicks where necessary. Bake ham further 30 minutes, brush frequently with remaining glaze. Serve with tamarillo sauce.

Glaze: Combine all ingredients in pan, stir over heat, without boiling, for 5 minutes, strain; cool.

Tamarillo Sauce: Cover tamarillos with boiling water, drain, peel away skins; chop tamarillos roughly. Combine tamarillos, sugar, water, onions, broth and wine in pan, simmer, covered, about 8 minutes or until pulpy. Push through sieve; discard pulp. Return liquid to pan, stir in blended cornstarch and extra water, stir over heat until mixture boils and thickens; simmer, uncovered, 2 minutes.

Serves 10 to 12.

▪ Recipe can be made a day ahead.
▪ Storage: Covered, in refrigerator.
▪ Freeze: Not suitable.
▪ Microwave: Glaze and tamarillo sauce suitable.

LEFT: From left: Pork with Prunes and Cabbage, Leek and Ham Pie with Cumberland Sauce.
ABOVE: Glazed Ham with Tamarillo Sauce.

HONEYED PORK AND PINEAPPLE CASSEROLE

2lb lean piece pork neck
3 tablespoons vegetable oil
1 medium onion, sliced
1 medium red bell
pepper, sliced
15oz can pineapple chunks in
heavy syrup
3 tablespoons light soy sauce
3 tablespoons Worcestershire sauce
½ cup tomato ketchup
4 teaspoons honey
3 tablespoons cornstarch
3 tablespoons water

Cut pork into 1¼ inch cubes. Heat oil in skillet, cook pork in batches until browned; transfer pork to ovenproof dish (6 cup capacity). Add onion and pepper to same skillet, cook, stirring, until onion is soft. Spoon onion mixture over pork.

Drain pineapple, reserve ⅓ cup syrup. Stir pineapple, reserved syrup, sauces, honey and blended cornstarch and water into pork mixture. Bake, covered, in 350˚F oven, stirring occasionally, about 40 minutes or until pork is tender and sauce is thickened.

Serves 4.

- Recipe can be made a day ahead.
- Storage: Covered, in refrigerator.
- Freeze: Suitable.
- Microwave: Suitable.

EGGPLANT AND PORK LOAF

You will need a total of 1½ cups fresh bread crumbs for this recipe. Spread crumbs on baking sheet, toast in 350˚F oven about 5 minutes.

¼ cup fresh bread crumbs, toasted
2½ medium (about 1½lb) eggplants
coarse (kosher) salt
½ cup olive oil
¾ cup grated Parmesan cheese
¾ cup fresh bread crumbs,
toasted, extra

FILLING
1½lb ground pork
1 egg
1 medium onion, chopped
2 cloves garlic, minced
3 tablespoons chopped fresh parsley
3 tablespoons tomato paste
½ small red bell pepper,
finely chopped
½ cup fresh bread crumbs, toasted

Lightly oil 5½ inch x 8½ inch loaf pan, sprinkle evenly with bread crumbs. Slice eggplants lengthways into ¼ inch slices, sprinkle with salt, stand 20 minutes. Rinse eggplants under cold water, drain, pat dry with absorbent paper. Heat oil in skillet, cook eggplant in batches until browned, drain well on absorbent paper.

Place a third of eggplants into prepared pan, sprinkle with half the cheese and half the extra bread crumbs. Top with half the filling, press down firmly. Repeat layering with eggplants, cheese, bread crumbs and filling, finishing with an eggplant layer. Bake, uncovered, in 350˚F oven about 1¼ hours or until loaf is cooked through. Drain off excess liquid, stand 15 minutes before serving.

Filling: Combine all ingredients in bowl, mix well.

Serves 6.

- Recipe can be made a day ahead.
- Storage: Covered, in refrigerator.
- Freeze: Not suitable.
- Microwave: Not suitable.

BRAISED RED CABBAGE WITH SAUSAGES AND APPLES

12 (about 2lb) thick pork sausages
3oz (¾ stick) butter
2 medium onions, finely chopped
1 small red cabbage, shredded
⅓ cup red wine vinegar
½ cup water
2 cloves
3 tablespoons sugar
¼ cup (½ stick) butter, extra
3 tablespoons dark brown sugar
2 medium apples, cored, sliced

Broil or pan-fry sausages until browned all over; drain. Heat butter in pan, add onions, cabbage, vinegar, water, cloves and sugar, simmer, uncovered, stirring occasionally, 40 minutes. Add sausages, cook, covered, 20 minutes.

Heat extra butter in skillet, add brown sugar, cook about 3 minutes or until bubbling. Add apples, cook, turning occasionally, about 10 minutes or until apples are browned and tender. Serve cabbage and sausages with apples.

Serves 6.

- Recipe can be made a day ahead.
- Storage: Covered, in refrigerator.
- Freeze: Not suitable.
- Microwave: Not suitable.

LEFT: Clockwise from front: Braised Red Cabbage with Sausages and Apples, Honeyed Pork and Pineapple Casserole, Eggplant and Pork Loaf.

JUNIPER BERRY PORK WITH GLAZED ONIONS

2 tablespoons (1/4 stick) butter
3 tablespoons olive oil
3lb lean pork cubes
1 medium carrot, sliced
1 medium onion, chopped
1 clove garlic, minced
1 teaspoon dried juniper berries, crushed
2 tablespoons paprika
3 tablespoons all-purpose flour
2/3 cup port wine
1/3 cup tomato puree
2 bay leaves
2 sprigs fresh thyme
2 sprigs fresh parsley
3 cups chicken broth

GLAZED ONIONS
1/2 cup dark seedless raisins
1/2 cup port wine
2 tablespoons (1/4 stick) butter
3 medium red onions, sliced
2 teaspoons sugar

Heat butter and oil in pan, cook pork in batches until browned all over; transfer pork to ovenproof dish (8 cup capacity).

Drain excess liquid from pan, reserving 4 teaspoons liquid in pan. Add carrot, onion, garlic and berries to pan, cook, stirring, until onion is soft. Add paprika and flour, cook, stirring, until combined.

Remove from heat, gradually stir in port wine, puree, herbs and broth, stir over heat until mixture boils and thickens slightly; pour over pork in dish. Bake, covered, in 350°F oven about 1 hour or until pork is tender; discard herbs; cool.

Cover dish, refrigerate several hours or overnight. Skim fat from pork mixture, transfer mixture to pan, stir over heat until hot. Serve topped with glazed onions.

Glazed Onions: Combine raisins and port wine in small bowl, cover, stand several hours or overnight.

Heat butter in skillet, add onions and sugar, cook, covered, over low heat about 45 minutes or until onions are lightly browned and very soft. Add undrained raisin mixture, stir until bubbling.

Serves 4 to 6.

- Recipe best prepared a day ahead.
- Storage: Covered, in refrigerator.
- Freeze: Pork mixture suitable.
- Microwave: Not suitable.

OSSO BUCCO

3lb (about 6 pieces) veal shanks
all-purpose flour
3 tablespoons olive oil
4 teaspoons olive oil, extra
2 medium onions, chopped
2 medium carrots, sliced
2 stalks celery, chopped
2 cloves garlic, minced
14 1/2 oz can tomatoes
1 bay leaf
2 teaspoons chopped fresh thyme
2/3 cup dry white wine
1 1/2 cups beef broth
3 tablespoons tomato paste

Toss veal in flour, shake away excess flour. Heat oil in skillet, cook veal in batches until well browned; drain on absorbent paper.

Heat extra oil in pan, add onions, carrots, celery and garlic, cook, stirring, until onions are soft. Stir in undrained crushed tomatoes, bay leaf, thyme, wine, broth and paste. Add veal to pan, simmer, covered, about 1 1/2 hours or until veal is tender, stirring occasionally.

Serves 4.

- Recipe can be made 2 days ahead.
- Storage: Covered, in refrigerator.
- Freeze: Suitable.
- Microwave: Not suitable.

GREEN PEA AND HAM RISOTTO

4 teaspoons olive oil
6 green onions, finely chopped
3 cups (1¼lb) arborio rice
1 cup dry white wine
5½ cups chicken broth
2½oz ham, chopped
2½oz sliced prosciutto, chopped
⅓ cup chopped fresh parsley
⅓ cup grated Parmesan cheese
½ cup frozen green peas, thawed

Heat oil in pan, add onions and rice, cook, stirring, until onions are soft. Add half the wine, stir over heat until evaporated. Stir in ¼ cup of the combined remaining wine and broth, cook, stirring, over low heat until liquid is absorbed.

Continue adding broth mixture very gradually, stirring until absorbed before next addition. Total cooking time should be about 30 minutes or until rice is tender. Stir in remaining ingredients, cook, stirring, until peas are tender and hot.

Serves 4 to 6.

■ Recipe best made just before serving.
■ Freeze: Not suitable.
■ Microwave: Not suitable.

LEFT: Osso Bucco.
BELOW: From back: Green Pea and Ham Risotto, Juniper Berry Pork with Glazed Onions.

Specialty dishes

Ingredients you don't use every day are the highlights of this section, with easy recipes showing how superb they can be. For entertaining, think of guinea hen and venison. Then, for a change in everyday eating, you can enjoy rabbit and often-overlooked delicacies such as tripe, brains, sweetbreads and chicken livers, all with their own special flavors.

BRAISED TRIPE WITH PANCETTA AND PASTA

½lb penne pasta
2lb honeycomb tripe
¼ cup (½ stick) butter
1 large onion, chopped
2 stalks celery, chopped
1 medium carrot, chopped
3½oz sliced pancetta, chopped
2 cloves garlic, minced
2 bay leaves
⅛ teaspoon cayenne pepper
15oz can tomato puree
4 cups chicken broth
2 tablespoons grated Parmesan cheese

Add pasta to large pan of boiling water, boil, uncovered, until just tender; drain. Cut tripe into thin strips, place in pan, cover with cold water, bring to boil; drain.

Heat butter in pan, add onion, celery, carrot and pancetta, cook, covered, until onion is soft. Add tripe, garlic, bay leaves, pepper, puree and broth. Bring to boil, skim surface, simmer, covered, 2 hours. Uncover pan, simmer further 30 minutes or until mixture is thickened slightly; discard bay leaves.

Place pasta in ovenproof dish (8 cup capacity), add tripe mixture, sprinkle with cheese. Bake, uncovered, in 400°F oven about 15 minutes or until browned and heated through.

Serves 6.

- ◼ Tripe mixture can be made a day ahead.
- ◼ Storage: Covered, in refrigerator.
- ◼ Freeze: Not suitable.
- ◼ Microwave: Pasta suitable.

VENISON BOURGUIGNONNE

2lb stewing venison
10 (about ½lb) pearl onions
2 cups dry red wine
½ cup port wine
1 clove garlic, minced
all-purpose flour
¼ cup olive oil
½ cup tomato puree
1 cup beef broth
2 bay leaves
7oz button mushrooms

Cut venison evenly into 1¼ inch cubes. Combine venison, onions, wine, port and garlic in bowl, cover, refrigerate several hours or overnight.

Drain venison, reserve onions and marinade separately. Pat venison dry with absorbent paper. Toss venison in flour; shake away excess flour. Heat oil in skillet, cook venison in batches until browned; drain on absorbent paper.

Return venison to pan, add reserved marinade, puree, broth and bay leaves, simmer, covered, 1 hour. Add reserved onions, cook about 1 hour or until venison is tender. Stir in mushrooms, simmer, covered, until mushrooms are tender; discard bay leaves.

Serves 4 to 6.

- ◼ Recipe can be made a day ahead.
- ◼ Storage: Covered, in refrigerator.
- ◼ Freeze: Suitable.
- ◼ Microwave: Not suitable.

RIGHT: From back: Venison Bourguignonne, Braised Tripe with Pancetta and Pasta.

RABBIT CUTLETS IN PRUNES AND BEER

2lb (about 8) rabbit cutlets
1 cup white vinegar
1½ cups water
1 cup (7oz) prunes
4 teaspoons vegetable oil
1 tablespoon butter
2 teaspoons grated fresh gingerroot
2 teaspoons dried juniper
   berries, crushed
2 large onions, chopped
2 tablespoons all-purpose flour
½ cup chicken broth
1 cup beer

Combine rabbit, vinegar and 1 cup of the water in bowl, cover, refrigerate overnight.

Combine prunes and remaining water in another bowl, cover, stand 1 hour. Drain rabbit, discard liquid.

Heat oil and butter in pan, cook rabbit in batches until browned; drain on absorbent paper. Add gingerroot, berries and onions to same pan, cook, stirring, until onions are soft. Add flour, cook, stirring, until combined. Remove from heat, gradually stir in undrained prunes, broth and beer, stir over heat until mixture boils and thickens slightly. Return rabbit to pan, simmer, covered, 40 minutes. Uncover, simmer further 15 minutes or until rabbit is tender.

Serves 4 to 6.

- Recipe can be made a day ahead.
- Storage: Covered, in refrigerator.
- Freeze: Suitable.
- Microwave: Not suitable.

CHICKEN LIVER FETTUCCINE

1lb chicken livers
5 green onions
1 bunch (about ½lb) fresh asparagus
4 teaspoons olive oil
2 slices bacon, chopped
2 cloves garlic, minced
3 tablespoons chopped fresh oregano
4 teaspoons chopped fresh parsley
1 teaspoon chicken bouillon powder
1 cup sour cream
1lb fettuccine pasta

Trim livers, cut livers in half. Cut onions and asparagus into ¾ inch lengths. Boil, steam or microwave asparagus until just tender, drain.

Heat oil in pan, add bacon and garlic, cook, stirring, until bacon is crisp. Add livers, cook, stirring, until livers change color. Add onions, asparagus, herbs, bouillon powder and cream, stir over heat until combined and heated through.

Meanwhile, add pasta to large pan of boiling water, boil, uncovered, until tender; drain. Serve sauce with pasta.

Serves 4.

- Recipe best made just before serving.
- Freeze: Not suitable.
- Microwave: Asparagus and pasta suitable.

BRAINS WITH ONION AND RED WINE SAUCE

12 sets lambs' brains
2 tablespoons vegetable oil
6 green onions, chopped
3 tablespoons shredded fresh sage

ONION AND RED WINE SAUCE
2 cups dry red wine
1 cup port wine
2 tablespoons red wine vinegar
1 medium red onion, sliced
2 cloves garlic, sliced
¾ cup sour cream
3oz (¾ stick) butter, chopped

Cover brains with cold water in bowl, stand 1 hour. Drain brains, peel away membrane. Cover brains with cold water in pan, bring to the boil, simmer, uncovered, about 2 minutes or until brains are just tender, drain; cool.

Heat oil in skillet, add brains, cook until browned all over. Add onions and sage, stir over heat until heated through. Serve with onion and red wine sauce.

Onion and Red Wine Sauce: Combine wine, port, vinegar, onion and garlic in pan. Boil, uncovered, until mixture is reduced by two-thirds. Stir in sour cream (mixture will appear curdled at this stage), simmer until sauce thickens slightly. Stir in butter gradually over low heat, stirring until mixture is combined between additions.

Serves 6.

- Recipe best made just before serving.
- Freeze: Not suitable.
- Microwave: Not suitable.

GUINEA HEN WITH BRAISED LETTUCE

1 tablespoon butter
4 teaspoons olive oil
2¼lb guinea hen
2 medium carrots, chopped
1 stalk celery, chopped
1 sprig fresh parsley
1 sprig fresh thyme
1 bay leaf
2 cups chicken broth
2 tablespoons all-purpose flour
2 tablespoons water

BRAISED LETTUCE
2 tablespoons (¼ stick) butter
1 small iceberg lettuce, chopped
1 small chicken bouillon cube

Heat butter and oil in large pan, add guinea hen, cook until browned all over; drain fat from pan. Add carrots, celery, herbs and a third of the broth, simmer, covered, 30 minutes. Turn guinea hen over, add half the remaining broth, simmer, covered, further 20 minutes. Remove guinea hen from pan; keep warm. Strain pan juices, reserve juices, discard pulp.

Heat reserved juices in pan with remaining broth, boil, uncovered, until reduced by half. Stir in blended flour and water, stir until sauce boils and thickens. Cut guinea hen into 4 pieces, serve with sauce and braised lettuce.

Braised Lettuce: Heat butter in skillet, add lettuce and crumbled bouillon cube, cook, stirring, until lettuce is just soft.

Serves 4.

- Recipe best made just before serving.
- Freeze: Not suitable.
- Microwave: Lettuce suitable.

LEFT: Clockwise from front: Rabbit Cutlets in Prunes and Beer, Brains with Onion and Red Wine Sauce, Chicken Liver Fettuccine.
ABOVE: Guinea Hen with Braised Lettuce.

SWEETBREADS, BELL PEPPER SALAD AND ONION RELISH

3lb veal sweetbreads
¼ cup white vinegar
¼ cup dry white wine
1 medium onion, sliced
2 bay leaves
all-purpose flour
2 eggs, lightly beaten
1 cup (2½oz) fresh bread crumbs
2 tablespoons olive oil

BELL PEPPER SALAD

2 large (about 1lb) red bell peppers
1 large (about ½lb) yellow bell pepper
4 teaspoons lemon juice
4 teaspoons olive oil
1 teaspoon chopped fresh parsley

ONION RELISH

¼ cup olive oil
5 medium (about 1½lb) onions, sliced
⅓ cup dry red wine
⅓ cup red wine vinegar
¾ cup sugar

Place sweetbreads in bowl, cover with cold water, stand 3 hours or overnight.

Drain sweetbreads, place in pan, cover with water. Add vinegar, wine, onion and bay leaves, simmer, uncovered, 1 minute.

Remove pan from heat, stand 30 minutes. Drain sweetbreads, place on tray, cover with cloth and heavy board, press down with weights, stand 1 hour. Remove weights, peel membrane and sinew from sweetbreads. Toss sweetbreads in flour, shake away excess flour. Dip into eggs, toss in bread crumbs to coat evenly. Heat oil in skillet, add sweetbreads, cook until browned. Serve with bell pepper salad and onion relish.

Bell Pepper Salad: Quarter peppers, remove seeds and membrane. Broil peppers skin-side-up until skin blisters and blackens. Peel away skin, slice peppers into thin strips. Combine peppers, juice, oil and parsley in bowl; mix well.

Onion Relish: Heat oil in pan, add onions, cook, covered, stirring occasionally, about 20 minutes or until soft. Add wine, vinegar and sugar, simmer, uncovered, about 45 minutes or until thick.

Serves 6.

- Sweetbreads and relish can be prepared a day ahead.
- Storage: Covered, in refrigerator.
- Freeze: Not suitable.
- Microwave: Not suitable.

RABBIT, MUSTARD AND TARRAGON RAGOUT

2lb rabbit cutlets
3 tablespoons butter
1 tablespoon butter, extra
12 (about 10oz) pearl onions, quartered
1¼ cups heavy cream
2 teaspoons drained green peppercorns
3 tablespoons chopped fresh tarragon

MARINADE

¼ cup French mustard
4 teaspoons hot English mustard
4 teaspoons seeded mustard
2 teaspoons cuminseed
¼ cup lemon juice
1 cup dry sherry

Cut rabbit cutlets in half through the bone. Combine rabbit with marinade in bowl, cover, refrigerate 3 hours or overnight.

Drain rabbit, reserve marinade. Heat butter in pan, add rabbit, cook until browned all over. Transfer rabbit and pan juices into ovenproof dish, bake, uncovered, in 350°F oven about 20 minutes or until rabbit is tender. Heat extra butter in same pan, add onions, cook, stirring, until soft. Stir in reserved marinade, cream, peppercorns and tarragon, simmer, uncovered, until sauce is thickened. Serve sauce over rabbit.

Marinade: Combine all ingredients in bowl; mix well.

Serves 4 to 6.

- Recipe best made just before serving.
- Freeze: Not suitable.
- Microwave: Not suitable.

DEEP-FRIED TRIPE AND ONION RINGS

1lb honeycomb tripe
1 bay leaf
1 stalk celery, chopped
1 small onion, chopped
1 medium carrot, chopped
1 large onion, extra
oil for deep-frying

BATTER
1 cup self-rising flour
1 teaspoon garlic salt
1 cup beer

TARTARE SAUCE
¾ cup mayonnaise
4 teaspoons chopped capers
1 small gherkin, chopped
4 teaspoons chopped fresh chives
2 tablespoons chopped fresh parsley
½ small red bell pepper,
    finely chopped

Place tripe in pan, cover with cold water, add bay leaf, celery, onion and carrot, simmer, covered, about 1 hour or until tripe is tender. Drain tripe; cool. Discard liquid and vegetables.

Cut tripe into ½ inch strips. Cut extra onion into ½ inch rings. Dip tripe and onion rings in batter, drain, deep-fry in batches in hot oil until lightly browned; drain on absorbent paper. Serve tripe hot with tartare sauce.

Batter: Sift flour and salt into bowl, stir in beer gradually; stir until smooth.

Tartare Sauce: Combine all ingredients in bowl; mix well.

Serves 4.

- Tripe can be prepared a day ahead. Tartare sauce can be made a day ahead.
- Storage: Covered, in refrigerator.
- Freeze: Not suitable.
- Microwave: Not suitable.

ABOVE LEFT: Sweetbreads, Bell Pepper Salad and Onion Relish.
RIGHT: From left: Rabbit, Mustard and Tarragon Ragout, Deep-Fried Tripe and Onion Rings.

Vegetarian

There's no limit to the ways you can turn vegetables into feasts of flavor in the comforting country tradition, creating main meals and appetizers for most occasions. You can choose from piping hot casseroles, cheesy crepes, a red onion flan, a tomato tart and more, including pasta. One pasta dish is smothered in the tastiest mustard sauce around!

SPICY VEGETABLE CURRY

3 large carrots
3 large potatoes
1 medium parsnip
2oz ghee
2 cloves garlic, minced
1 teaspoon ground coriander
1 teaspoon ground cumin
1 teaspoon ground cardamom
1 teaspoon turmeric
2 teaspoons grated fresh gingerroot
1 teaspoon sambal oelek
1 medium onion, chopped
1¾ cups canned unsweetened coconut milk
¼ medium (about ½lb) cauliflower, chopped
½lb broccoli, chopped
½lb button mushrooms, halved
1 cup water

Chop carrots, potatoes and parsnip into 1¼ inch pieces. Heat ghee in pan, add garlic, spices, gingerroot, sambal oelek and onion, cook, stirring, until onion is soft. Add carrots and coconut milk, simmer, covered, 15 minutes. Add potatoes and parsnip, simmer, covered, until vegetables are tender. Add cauliflower, broccoli, mushrooms and water, simmer, covered, until vegetables are tender.

Serves 4.

■ Recipe can be made a day ahead.
■ Storage: Covered, in refrigerator.
■ Freeze: Not suitable.
■ Microwave: Suitable.

CHEESY BUCKWHEAT CREPES

½ cup whole-wheat flour
½ cup buckwheat flour
2 eggs
1½ cups milk
10oz ricotta cheese
¾ cup grated cheddar cheese

FILLING
4 teaspoons olive oil
1 medium red onion, chopped
1 clove garlic, minced
1 teaspoon cuminseed
1 medium carrot, chopped
1 medium potato, chopped
2 medium zucchini, chopped
5oz small yellow pattypan squash, chopped
1 medium red bell pepper, chopped
½ teaspoon sambal oelek
1 teaspoon ground coriander
14½oz can tomatoes
¾ cup tomato puree

Sift flours into bowl, gradually whisk in combined eggs and milk. Pour 3 to 4 tablespoons of batter into heated greased heavy-based crepe pan; cook until lightly browned underneath. Turn, brown other side. Repeat with remaining batter. You will need 12 crepes for this recipe.

Grease shallow ovenproof dish (10 cup capacity). Spread 2 tablespoons of ricotta cheese over half of each crepe, top with ¼ cup of filling, roll crepes, place seam-side-down in single layer in prepared dish. Spread remaining filling over crepes, sprinkle with cheddar cheese. Bake, uncovered, in 350°F oven about 30 minutes or until cheese is browned and crèpes are heated through.
Filling: Heat oil in pan, add onion, garlic and seeds, cook, stirring, until onion is soft. Add vegetables, sambal oelek and coriander, cook, stirring, until vegetables are tender. Stir in undrained crushed tomatoes and puree, simmer, uncovered, until thickened.

Serves 4.

■ Recipe can be prepared a day ahead.
■ Storage: Covered, in refrigerator.
■ Freeze: Unfilled crepes suitable.
■ Microwave: Filling suitable.

RIGHT: From left: Spicy Vegetable Curry, Cheesy Buckwheat Crepes.

GARBANZO BEAN AND TOMATO CASSEROLE

1 cup (7oz) dried garbanzo beans
1 medium (about 10oz) eggplant
coarse (kosher) salt
4 teaspoons olive oil
2 medium onions, sliced
2 cloves garlic, minced
10 (about 26oz) tomatoes, chopped
3 tablespoons tomato paste
1 cup vegetable broth
½ medium green bell pepper, chopped
½ medium yellow bell pepper, chopped
2 medium zucchini, sliced
5oz mushrooms, quartered
1 teaspoon sugar
3 tablespoons chopped fresh basil
½ cup grated Parmesan cheese

Place garbanzo beans in bowl, cover with water, cover, stand overnight.

Drain garbanzo beans, rinse, add to pan of boiling water, simmer, uncovered, about 45 minutes or until just tender; rinse, drain. Cut eggplant into ¾ inch pieces, sprinkle with salt; stand 30 minutes. Rinse eggplant under cold water, drain, pat dry with absorbent paper.

Heat oil in pan, add eggplant, onions and garlic, cook, stirring, until onions are soft. Add tomatoes, paste and broth, simmer, covered, until tomatoes are pulpy. Stir in peppers, zucchini, mushrooms and sugar, simmer, covered, until vegetables are just tender. Stir in garbanzo beans, basil and cheese, stir until hot.

Serves 6.

- Recipe can be made a day ahead.
- Storage: Covered, in refrigerator.
- Freeze: Not suitable.
- Microwave: Suitable.

RED ONION FLAN

½ teaspoon caraway seeds
1 teaspoon ground coriander
1¼ cups all-purpose flour
½ cup grated Parmesan cheese
3oz (¾ stick) butter, chopped
1 egg yolk
4 teaspoons water, approximately
½ cup grated Parmesan cheese, extra
½ cup sour cream
2 eggs, lightly beaten

RED ONION FILLING
4 teaspoons olive oil
3 tablespoons butter
4 medium (about 1¼lb) red onions, sliced
1 clove garlic, minced
4 teaspoons dark brown sugar
4 teaspoons red wine vinegar

Lightly grease 9 inch flan pan. Heat seeds in dry pan. When seeds begin to pop, add coriander, cook, stirring, until fragrant; cool. Sift flour into bowl, stir in caraway mixture and cheese, rub in butter. Add egg yolk and enough water to make ingredients cling together. Knead dough gently on floured surface until smooth; cover, refrigerate 30 minutes.

Roll dough between sheets of baking paper until large enough to line prepared pan. Lift pastry into pan, ease into side, trim edge. Place pan on baking sheet, line pastry with paper, fill with dried beans or rice. Bake in 375°F oven 12 minutes, remove paper and beans, bake further 8 minutes or until browned; cool.

Sprinkle extra cheese into flan case, top with filling; pour over combined cream and eggs. Bake in 350°F oven about 25 minutes or until set.

Red Onion Filling: Heat oil and butter in skillet, add onions and garlic, cook, covered, over low heat about 10 minutes or until onions are soft. Stir in sugar and vinegar, cook, uncovered, further 10 minutes or until very soft; cool.

Serves 6.

- Recipe can be made a day ahead.
- Storage: Covered, in refrigerator.
- Freeze: Not suitable.
- Microwave: Not suitable.

PASTA WITH CAULIFLOWER MUSTARD SAUCE

1lb spinach fettuccine pasta
4 teaspoons olive oil
1 tablespoon butter
2 cloves garlic, minced
2 tablespoons grated fresh gingerroot
4 teaspoons chopped fresh thyme
1½ stalks celery, chopped
½ medium (about 1¼lb) cauliflower, chopped
¼ cup French mustard
4 teaspoons seeded mustard
3 tablespoons English mustard
1 teaspoon ground cumin
⅓ cup chopped fresh cilantro
¼ cup fresh lemon juice
1 cup dry white wine
2⅓ cups heavy cream
¾ cup Brazil nuts, toasted, chopped
¾ cup shredded mozzarella cheese

Add pasta to large pan of boiling water, boil, uncovered, until just tender; drain.

Meanwhile heat oil and butter in pan, add garlic, gingerroot, thyme, celery and cauliflower, cook, stirring, 3 minutes. Stir in mustards, cumin, cilantro, juice, wine and cream, simmer, uncovered, until cauliflower is tender and liquid is reduced by half. Stir in nuts and cheese, stir over heat until combined. Serve with pasta.

Serves 4 to 6.

- Recipe best made just before serving.
- Freeze: Not suitable.
- Microwave: Pasta suitable.

LEFT: Clockwise from left: Red Onion Flan, Pasta with Cauliflower Mustard Sauce, Garbanzo Bean and Tomato Casserole.

SPINACH SEASONED TOMATO TART

2 cups all-purpose flour
¼ cup (½ stick) butter
1 egg yolk
⅓ cup water, approximately
6 medium (about 1½lb) tomatoes , peeled
2 teaspoons coarse (kosher) salt
6 eggs, lightly beaten
¾ cup heavy cream
½ cup grated Parmesan cheese

SPINACH SEASONING
2 tablespoons (¼ stick) butter
1 medium (about ¾lb) leek, sliced
10oz package frozen spinach, thawed
¼lb mushrooms, chopped
1 cup (2½oz) fresh bread crumbs
3 tablespoons chopped fresh basil
1 teaspoon seeded mustard

Grease deep 10 inch loose-based flan pan. Sift flour into bowl, rub in butter, stir in egg yolk and enough water to make ingredients cling together; cover, refrigerate for 30 minutes.

Roll pastry on floured surface large enough to line base and side of prepared pan. Lift pastry into pan, ease into side, trim edge. Place pan on baking sheet, line pastry with paper, fill with dried beans or rice. Bake in 375°F oven 15 minutes, remove paper, bake further 15 minutes or until pastry is browned and crisp; cool.

Cut tops from tomatoes, reserve tops; scoop out seeds and pulp; reserve pulp for another use. Sprinkle tomato shells with salt, place upside-down on wire rack over tray, stand 30 minutes; pat dry with absorbent paper.

Fill tomatoes with spinach seasoning, replace tops, press down gently. Place tomatoes into pastry case. Pour over combined eggs and cream; sprinkle with cheese. Bake in 350°F oven about 1¼ hours or until set.

Spinach Seasoning: Heat butter in skillet, add leek, spinach and mushrooms, cook, stirring, until liquid is evaporated. Stir in bread crumbs, basil and mustard.

Serves 6.

■ Recipe best made just before serving.
■ Freeze: Not suitable.
■ Microwave: Not suitable.

SATAY-STYLE TOFU AND SPICY VEGETABLES

¾lb package firm tofu
¼ cup light soy sauce
1 teaspoon fish sauce
4 teaspoons sugar
½ teaspoon grated lime zest
2 teaspoons fresh lime juice
3 tablespoons vegetable oil
1 medium red onion, chopped
1 clove garlic, minced
3 tablespoons chopped fresh lemon grass
1 teaspoon sambal oelek
1 teaspoon turmeric
1 teaspoon ground cumin
4 teaspoons paprika
⅓ cup roasted unsalted peanuts
1 medium carrot, chopped
1 medium green bell pepper, chopped
3 small zucchini, sliced
¾ medium (about 1½lb) cauliflower, chopped
¾ cup canned unsweetened coconut milk
1 cup vegetable broth
⅓ cup peanut butter

Wrap tofu in absorbent paper, squeeze out excess liquid. Cut tofu into ½ inch x 1½ inch pieces. Combine tofu, sauces, sugar, zest and juice in bowl, cover, refrigerate overnight.

Heat oil in pan, add onion, garlic, lemon grass, spices and peanuts, cook, stirring, until onion is soft. Add carrot, pepper, zucchini, cauliflower, coconut milk, broth and peanut butter, simmer, covered, until vegetables are tender. Add tofu mixture, stir until heated through. Serve with rice, if desired.

Serves 4.

■ Recipe can be prepared a day ahead.
■ Storage: Covered, in refrigerator.
■ Freeze: Not suitable.
■ Microwave: Suitable.

WHOLE-WHEAT PUMPKIN AND VEGETABLE SLICE

1 cup all-purpose flour
1 cup whole-wheat flour
½ cup (1 stick) butter, chopped
2 egg yolks
¼ cup water, approximately
1½ cups cooked rice
1½ cups (7oz) grated smoked cheese

VEGETABLE FILLING
½lb broccoli, chopped
2 tablespoons (¼ stick) butter
1 medium (about ¾lb) leek, sliced
1 clove garlic, minced
½ small red bell pepper, chopped
½ small green bell pepper, chopped
½ x 8oz can whole-kernel corn, drained
1 tablespoon curry powder
1 teaspoon ground cumin

PUMPKIN FILLING
**2 cups cooked mashed pumpkin
squash
6 eggs, lightly beaten**

Grease shallow 8 inch x 12 inch baking pan. Sift flours into bowl, rub in butter; add egg yolks and enough water to make ingredients cling together. Knead dough gently on lightly floured surface until smooth. Cover, refrigerate 30 minutes.

Roll pastry on floured surface large enough to line base and sides of prepared pan; lift into pan. Make a double edge of pastry from scraps, join with a little egg white. Trim edges evenly, pinch edges of pastry decoratively.

Line pastry with paper, fill with dried beans or rice. Bake in 375°F oven 15 minutes, remove paper and beans, bake further 12 minutes or until pastry is lightly browned; cool.

Spoon rice into pastry case, top with half the vegetable filling; pour over half the pumpkin filling. Top with remaining vegetable filling, cheese, then remaining pumpkin filling. Bake, uncovered, in 350°F oven about 30 minutes or until filling is firm to touch.

Vegetable Filling: Boil, steam or microwave broccoli until tender, drain; pat dry with absorbent paper.

Heat butter in skillet, add leek, garlic and peppers, cook, stirring, until leek is soft. Add corn, curry powder and cumin, cook, stirring, until fragrant; stir in broccoli.
Pumpkin Filling: Add squash to dry skillet, cook, stirring, until squash is thick and excess liquid is evaporated; cool. Combine eggs and pumpkin in bowl.

Serves 6 to 8.

- Recipe can be made a day ahead.
- Storage: Covered, in refrigerator.
- Freeze: Not suitable.
- Microwave: Broccoli suitable.

*LEFT: Spinach Seasoned Tomato Tart.
ABOVE: Clockwise from right: Satay-Style Tofu and Spicy Vegetables, Whole-Wheat Pumpkin and Vegetable Slice.*

BAKED POLENTA SLICE WITH THREE CHEESES

4 cups water
1¼ cups (7½oz) yellow cornmeal
10oz mozzarella cheese, thinly sliced

TOMATO AND BASIL FILLING
4 teaspoons olive oil
2 small onions, finely chopped
3 cloves garlic, minced
¼ teaspoon sambal oelek
10 pitted black olives, halved
⅓ cup chopped fresh basil
2 medium (about 8oz) tomatoes,
  finely chopped
¾ cup dry white wine

TOPPING
1 tablespoon butter
½ small leek, sliced
10oz button mushrooms, sliced
½ cup pine nuts, toasted
¼lb gorgonzola cheese, crumbled
1 cup (¼lb) grated cheddar cheese

Lightly grease shallow 8 inch x 12 inch baking pan. Bring water to boil in saucepan, gradually add cornmeal, simmer, uncovered, about 15 minutes or until thick, stirring occasionally. Spread mixture evenly into prepared pan, cool.

Spread tomato and basil filling over polenta, spoon over topping. Cover with overlapping slices of mozzarella cheese. Bake, uncovered, in 375°F oven about 20 minutes or until cheese is lightly browned.
Tomato and Basil Filling: Heat oil in pan, add onions and garlic, cook, stirring, until onions are soft. Add sambal oelek, olives, basil and tomatoes, cook, stirring, 5 minutes. Add wine, simmer, uncovered, until mixture is thickened. Blend or process mixture until smooth.
Topping: Heat butter in skillet, add leek and mushrooms, cook, stirring, until vegetables are soft. Remove from heat, stir in nuts, and gorgonzola and cheddar cheeses; mix well.

Serves 4.

- Polenta can be cooked a day ahead.
- Storage: Covered, in refrigerator.
- Freeze: Not suitable.
- Microwave: Polenta and topping suitable.

PASTA WITH OKRA, TOMATOES AND OLIVES

3 tablespoons olive oil
1 medium onion, chopped
2 cloves garlic, minced
28oz can tomatoes
3 tablespoons tomato paste
1 cup vegetable broth
3 tablespoons chopped fresh
  marjoram
½ cup sliced pitted black olives
1 teaspoon sugar
10oz small okra
14oz penne pasta

Heat oil in pan, add onion and garlic, cook, stirring, until onion is soft. Add undrained crushed tomatoes, paste, broth, marjoram, olives and sugar; simmer, uncovered, until slightly thickened. Add okra, simmer 5 minutes or until okra are tender.

Add pasta to large pan of boiling water, boil, uncovered, until just tender; drain. Serve sauce with pasta.

Serves 4.

- Recipe best made just before serving.
- Freeze: Not suitable.
- Microwave: Suitable.

LIMA BEAN CASSEROLE WITH SCALLOP POTATO TOP

2⅔ cups (1lb) dried lima beans
4 teaspoons olive oil
2 large onions, sliced
2 cloves garlic, minced
2 teaspoons all-purpose flour
2 cups vegetable broth
14½oz can tomatoes
½ cup tomato puree
¼ cup tomato paste
1 teaspoon sugar
2 medium carrots, chopped
1 stalk celery, chopped
5 (about 10oz) new potatoes
1 tablespoon butter, melted
½ teaspoon cuminseed

Place beans in bowl, cover well with water, cover, stand overnight.

Drain beans, add to large pan of boiling water, boil, uncovered, about 1 hour or until tender; drain.

Heat oil in pan, add onions and garlic, cook, stirring, until onions are soft. Add flour, cook, stirring, until combined. Remove from heat, gradually stir in broth, undrained crushed tomatoes, puree, paste, sugar, carrots and celery. Simmer, covered, until carrots are tender; stir in beans. Cut potatoes into ¹⁄₁₆ inch slices.

Pour bean mixture into ovenproof dish (8 cup capacity). Top with potato slices, brush with butter, sprinkle with cuminseed. Bake, uncovered, in 375°F oven about 40 minutes or until potato slices are browned and tender.

Serves 6.

- Recipe can be made a day ahead.
- Storage: Covered, in refrigerator.
- Freeze: Not suitable.
- Microwave: Beans suitable.

RIGHT: Clockwise from top left: Pasta with Okra, Tomatoes and Olives, Lima Bean Casserole with Scallop Potato Top, Baked Polenta Slice with Three Cheeses.

MUSHROOM LASAGNE

¼ cup (½ stick) butter
½ cup all-purpose flour
2½ cups milk
¼ cup grated Parmesan cheese
1 egg, lightly beaten
3 tablespoons chopped fresh basil
6 sheets no boil lasagne pasta
3 tablespoons fresh bread crumbs
4 teaspoons grated Parmesan
   cheese, extra
3 tablespoons pine nuts, chopped
¼ teaspoon paprika

FILLING
2 tablespoons (¼ stick) butter
1½lb flat mushrooms, sliced
1 medium (about ¾lb) leek, chopped
2 cloves garlic, minced

Melt butter in pan, stir in flour, stir over heat until bubbling. Remove from heat, gradually stir in milk, stir over heat until mixture boils and thickens. Cool slightly, stir in cheese, egg and basil.

Spread one-third of the filling over base of ovenproof dish (6 cup capacity). Cover with 3 lasagne sheets, half the remaining filling, half the cheese sauce, then remain- ing lasagne sheets. Top with remaining filling and cheese sauce. Sprinkle with combined bread crumbs, extra cheese, nuts and paprika. Bake lasagne in 350°F oven about 40 minutes or until well browned and hot.

Filling: Heat butter in skillet, add mush- rooms, leek and garlic, cook, stirring, until mushrooms and leek are soft; drain.

Serves 4.

■ Recipe can be prepared a day ahead.
■ Storage: Covered, in refrigerator.
■ Freeze: Not suitable.
■ Microwave: Sauce and filling suitable.

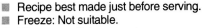

RATATOUILLE CALZONE

1 package (¼oz) active dry yeast
1 teaspoon sugar
⅓ cup warm water
¼ cup warm milk
1½ cups all-purpose flour
3 tablespoons olive oil
1 egg, lightly beaten

SAUCE
⅓ bunch (7oz) spinach
¼ cup (½ stick) butter
¼ cup all-purpose flour
1 cup milk

RATATOUILLE
1 small eggplant
coarse (kosher) salt
¼ cup olive oil
½ small green bell pepper, chopped
½ small red bell pepper, chopped
1 medium zucchini, chopped
1 small red onion, sliced
1 clove garlic, minced
3 tablespoons tomato paste
4 teaspoons chopped fresh basil

Combine yeast, sugar, water and milk in bowl, cover, stand in warm place about 10 minutes or until mixture is frothy. Sift flour into large bowl, add yeast mixture and oil, mix to a firm dough. Turn dough onto floured surface, knead about 5 minutes or until dough is smooth and elastic. Return dough to greased bowl, cover, stand in warm place about 1 hour or until dough is doubled in size.

Turn dough onto floured surface, knead until smooth. Roll dough into 12 inch circle, place on greased baking sheet. Spread sauce over dough, leaving ¾ inch border. Spoon ratatouille evenly over half the sauce. Brush edge of dough with egg, fold dough in half, pinch edges firmly together to seal.

Bake in 375°F oven 10 minutes, reduce heat to 350°F, bake further 10 minutes or until calzone is browned and cooked.
Sauce: Boil, steam or microwave spinach until wilted; drain well, chop finely. Melt butter in pan, stir in flour, stir over heat until bubbling. Remove from heat, gradually stir in milk, stir over heat until sauce boils and thickens, stir in spinach; cool.
Ratatouille: Cut eggplant into ½ inch cubes, sprinkle with salt; stand 30 minutes. Rinse eggplant under cold water, pat dry with absorbent paper. Heat oil in skillet, add eggplant, cook, stirring, until browned. Add peppers, zucchini, onion, garlic and paste, cook, stirring, until vegetables are tender, stir in basil; cool.
Serves 4.

- Recipe best made just before serving.
- Freeze: Not suitable.
- Microwave: Spinach and sauce suitable.

BAKED SPINACH GNOCCHI WITH TOMATO SAUCE

1 bunch (1¼lb) spinach
1lb ricotta cheese
1 cup (2½oz) grated Parmesan cheese
2 eggs, lightly beaten
¼ teaspoon ground nutmeg
all-purpose flour
¼ cup grated Parmesan cheese, extra

TOMATO SAUCE
4 teaspoons olive oil
1 small onion, chopped
1 clove garlic, minced
14½oz can tomatoes
3 tablespoons tomato paste
3 tablespoons chopped fresh basil
1 teaspoon sugar

Boil, steam or microwave spinach until just wilted; rinse under cold water, drain well, chop finely. Combine spinach, cheeses, eggs and nutmeg in bowl. Toss 3 level tablespoons of mixture in flour, shape into an oval. Repeat with remaining mixture. Add gnocchi to pan of simmering water, a few at a time, simmer, uncovered, 2 minutes. Remove with slotted spoon, drain on absorbent paper.

Place gnocchi in single layer in greased, shallow ovenproof dish (8 cup capacity), spoon over tomato sauce, sprinkle with extra cheese. Bake, uncovered, in 375°F oven about 30 minutes or until hot.
Tomato Sauce: Heat oil in pan, add onion and garlic, cook, stirring, until onion is soft. Stir in undrained crushed tomatoes, paste, basil and sugar, simmer, uncovered until sauce is thickened.
Serves 6.

- Recipe can be made a day ahead.
- Storage: Covered, in refrigerator.
- Freeze: Not suitable.
- Microwave: Spinach, gnocchi and tomato sauce suitable.

FAR LEFT: From back: Mushroom Lasagne, Ratatouille Calzone.
LEFT: Baked Spinach Gnocchi with Tomato Sauce.

Desserts

For truly luscious comfort food, look no further than our gorgeous desserts with the old-world appeal that brings rave reviews every time they appear on your table. They're perfect for today, a scrumptious mix of hot and hearty puddings or cool, light and refreshing treats. Every spoonful is destined to be a sweet experience to remember.

HOT BLACKBERRY SOUFFLES

½lb blackberries
¼ cup water
½ cup granulated sugar
4 egg whites

Heat blackberries and water in pan, simmer, uncovered, until blackberries are soft and pulpy. Add sugar, stir over heat, without boiling, until sugar is dissolved. Simmer, uncovered, without stirring, until mixture is thick and syrupy.

Beat egg whites in small bowl with electric mixer until soft peaks form. Gradually pour hot blackberry mixture onto egg whites while motor is operating. Spoon mixture into 4 ovenproof dishes (1 cup capacity), place on baking sheet. Bake in 350°F oven about 15 minutes or until souffles are puffed and browned; serve immediately. Dust with sifted confectioners' sugar, if desired.

Serves 4.

- Souffles must be made just before serving.
- Freeze: Not suitable.
- Microwave: Not suitable.

PASSION FRUIT AND BERRY MERINGUES

3 egg whites
¾ cup superfine sugar

PASSION FRUIT CREAM
5 passion fruit
2 teaspoons confectioners' sugar
½lb package mascarpone cheese

RASPBERRY SAUCE
1 cup (5oz) raspberries
3 egg yolks
¼ cup granulated sugar
2 tablespoons grated lemon zest
3 tablespoons fresh lemon juice
3oz (¾ stick) unsalted butter, chopped

Beat egg whites in small bowl with electric mixer until soft peaks form. Gradually beat in sugar, beat until dissolved between each addition. Drop 3 level tablespoons of mixture about 1¼ inches apart onto foil-covered baking sheets. Bake in 250°F oven about 1 hour or until dry. Cool in oven with door ajar. Serve meringues with passion fruit cream and raspberry sauce.

Passion Fruit Cream: Strain passion fruit pulp, reserve ¼ cup juice and 4 teaspoons seeds. Combine reserved juice and seeds, sugar and cheese in bowl; mix well.

Raspberry Sauce: Push raspberries through fine sieve; discard seeds. Combine raspberry puree, yolks, sugar, zest, juice and butter in heatproof bowl. Stand bowl over pan of simmering water, whisk constantly about 10 minutes or until butter is melted and mixture is thickened slightly. Transfer to another bowl; cool.

Serves 6.

- Meringues and passion fruit cream can be made a day ahead. Raspberry sauce best made just before serving.
- Storage: Meringues, airtight container. Passion fruit cream, covered, in refrigerator.
- Freeze: Not suitable.
- Microwave: Not suitable.

RIGHT: From back: Hot Blackberry Souffles, Passion Fruit and Berry Meringues.

ALMOND, HONEY AND DATE PIE

1¼ cups all-purpose flour
**1 cup (¼lb) packaged ground
   almonds**
¼ cup granulated sugar
3oz (¾ stick) butter, chopped
1 egg

FILLING
**1 cup (¼lb) packaged ground
   almonds**
¼ cup dark brown sugar
⅓ cup honey
1 tablespoon grated lemon zest
¾ cup (1½ sticks) butter, chopped
4 eggs
½ cup chopped pitted dates

Grease 9 inch flan pan. Sift flour into bowl, stir in nuts and sugar, rub in butter, add egg, mix until well combined and mixture forms a ball. Press mixture evenly over base and side of prepared pan. Place pan on baking sheet, pour filling into pan, bake in 300°F oven about 45 minutes or until firm; cool.

Filling: Blend or process nuts, sugar, honey and zest until combined. Add butter and eggs gradually, blending until combined between additions. Transfer mixture to bowl, stir in dates.

Serves 6 to 8.

- Recipe can be made 2 days ahead.
- Storage: Covered, in refrigerator.
- Freeze: Suitable.
- Microwave: Not suitable.

CHERRY CLAFOUTI

**2 x 14oz cans pitted black cherries,
   drained**
¾ cup milk
2 eggs
2 teaspoons vanilla extract
⅓ cup confectioners' sugar
⅓ cup all-purpose flour
1 teaspoon mixed spice

Lightly grease 10½ inch pie dish. Spread cherries over base of prepared dish. Beat milk, eggs, extract and sifted sugar in small bowl with electric mixer until combined, gradually beat in sifted flour and spice, beat until smooth. Pour batter over cherries. Bake in 350°F oven about 50 minutes or until set and browned. Serve warm or cold.

Serves 6.

- Recipe can be made a day ahead.
- Storage: Covered, in refrigerator.
- Freeze: Not suitable.
- Microwave: Not suitable.

WINTER FRUIT SALAD WITH BANANA BREAD

¾ cup fresh orange juice
¾ cup water
⅓ cup sweet white wine
¼ cup brandy
1 cinnamon stick
12 (7oz) dried figs
12 (5½oz) dried peaches
6 (3½oz) dried pears
18 (3oz) dried apricots

BANANA BREAD
3oz (¾ stick) butter
½ cup granulated sugar
1 egg
¾ cup all-purpose flour
¼ cup self-rising flour
½ teaspoon ground cinnamon
2 ripe bananas, thinly sliced
½ cup chopped macadamias

HONEY CREAM
½ cup whipping cream
3 tablespoons honey
½ cup plain yogurt

Heat juice, water, wine, brandy and cinnamon in pan, stir in fruit. Simmer, covered, about 5 minutes or until fruit is soft. Stand fruit mixture 15 minutes, remove and discard cinnamon stick. Serve fruit with warm banana bread and honey cream.

Banana Bread: Grease 3 inch x 10½ inch baking pan, line base with paper, grease paper. Beat butter and sugar in small bowl with electric mixer until light and fluffy, add egg, beat until combined. Stir in sifted dry ingredients, bananas and nuts. Spread mixture into prepared pan, bake in 350°F oven about 55 minutes or until browned and firm. Turn onto wire rack; cool to warm.

Honey Cream: Beat cream and honey in small bowl until soft peaks form, fold in yogurt, cover, refrigerate 1 hour.

Serves 6.

- Recipe can be made a day ahead.
- Storage: Covered, in refrigerator.
- Freeze: Banana bread suitable.
- Microwave: Fruit suitable.

*LEFT: Clockwise from front left: Winter Fruit
Salad with Banana Bread, Cherry Clafouti,
Almond, Honey and Date Pie.*

CHARLOTTE LOUISE

1 cup water
¼ cup granulated sugar
¼ cup Grand Marnier
12 sponge finger cookies

FILLING
1 teaspoon unflavored gelatin
3 tablespoons water
½lb semisweet chocolate, melted
3 tablespoons butter, melted
2 teaspoons grated orange zest
2⅓ cups whipping cream

Line charlotte mold (7 cup capacity) with plastic wrap. Combine water and sugar in pan, stir over heat, without boiling, until sugar is dissolved. Boil, uncovered, 5 minutes, stir in liqueur; cool. Dip each cookie into syrup, line side of prepared mold with cookies. Pour filling into mold, cover, refrigerate 3 hours or overnight.
Filling: Sprinkle gelatin over water in cup, stand in small pan of simmering water, stir until dissolved. Combine gelatin mixture, chocolate, butter and zest in bowl. Beat cream in small bowl with electric mixer until soft peaks form; fold into chocolate mixture in 2 batches.

Serves 6.

- Recipe best made a day ahead.
- Storage: Covered, in refrigerator.
- Freeze: Not suitable.
- Microwave: Chocolate, butter and gelatin suitable.

BAKED GINGER APPLES

6 large (about 2½lb) apples
½ cup golden raisins
1 tablespoon butter, softened
4 teaspoons chopped glace gingerroot
¼ teaspoon ground cinnamon
½ cup sour cream

SAUCE
¾ cup granulated sugar
⅓ cup water
½ cup fresh orange juice

Core apples, replace small amount of core in base. Slit skin around center of apples. Combine golden raisins, butter, gingerroot and cinnamon in bowl. Press mixture into apples. Place apples in shallow 8 inch x 12 inch baking pan. Bake, uncovered, in 350°F oven 30 minutes. Pour sauce over apples, reduce heat to 300°F, bake, uncovered, 50 minutes or until apples are soft. Remove apples, stir sour cream into sauce, serve with sauce.
Sauce: Combine sugar and water in pan, stir over heat, without boiling, until sugar is dissolved. Boil, uncovered, without stirring, about 5 minutes or until syrup is golden brown. Add juice, stir over heat until toffee is dissolved.

Serves 6.

- Recipe best made just before serving.
- Freeze: Not suitable.
- Microwave: Apples suitable.

CHEESE STRUDEL

5oz ricotta cheese
7oz packaged cream cheese
2 teaspoons grated lemon zest
1 tablespoon fresh lemon juice
½ cup granulated sugar
2 eggs, separated
½ cup golden raisins
⅓ cup packaged ground almonds
½ cup fresh bread crumbs
10 sheets phyllo pastry
3oz (¾ stick) butter, melted

Beat ricotta and cream cheese in bowl with electric mixer until smooth. Beat in zest, juice and sugar, then egg yolks 1 at a time. Fold in golden raisins, nuts and bread crumbs.

Brush a sheet of pastry with some of the butter, place another sheet half way down the narrow side to form a large square. Brush with butter and layer remaining pastry sheets and butter in same way.

Beat egg whites in bowl until soft peaks form, fold into cheese mixture. Spoon mixture along the long side of pastry, leaving 2 inch border at ends. Roll once, fold in ends and roll up to form a log shape. Place on greased baking sheet, brush with any remaining butter. Bake in 350°F oven about 35 minutes or until pastry is puffed and browned.

Serves 8.

- Recipe best made just before serving.
- Freeze: Not suitable.
- Microwave: Not suitable.

RIGHT: Clockwise from back: Charlotte Louise, Cheese Strudel, Baked Ginger Apples.

CHOCOLATE WHISKY FUDGE CAKE

This is a very moist, fudgy cake which may sink slightly on cooling.

¾ cup (1½ sticks) unsalted butter
¾ cup granulated sugar
3 eggs, separated
¼ cup whisky
4 teaspoons vanilla extract
7oz semisweet chocolate, melted
1 cup self-rising flour

Grease deep 9 inch round springform pan; line base with paper, grease paper.

Beat butter and ½ cup of the sugar in small bowl with electric mixer until light and fluffy. Beat in egg yolks, whisky and extract, beat until combined. Beat in cooled chocolate. Transfer mixture to large bowl, fold in sifted flour.

Beat egg whites in small bowl with electric mixer until soft peaks form, gradually beat in remaining sugar, beat until sugar is dissolved. Stir quarter of the egg white mixture into chocolate mixture, then fold in remaining egg white mixture. Spoon chocolate mixture into prepared pan. Bake, covered with foil, in 325°F oven 30 minutes. Uncover, bake further 1 hour or until cake is cooked through. Run a knife around edge of cake, leave cake to cool in pan.

Serves 8.

- Recipe can be made a day ahead.
- Storage: Airtight container.
- Freeze: Suitable.
- Microwave: Not suitable.

BLUEBERRY AND APPLE BROWN BETTY

3 large (about 1¼lb) apples, peeled, cored, sliced
⅓ cup granulated sugar
½ cup water
3 cloves
2 x 26½oz cans blueberries, drained
1 teaspoon grated lemon zest
3 tablespoons fresh lemon juice
1 teaspoon ground cinnamon
2 cups (5oz) fresh bread crumbs
3oz (¾ stick) butter, melted
½ cup shredded coconut

Grease shallow ovenproof dish (6 cup capacity). Combine apples, sugar, water and cloves in pan, simmer, covered, until apples are just tender. Strain apples, discard liquid; cool apples.

Combine blueberries, zest, juice and cinnamon in bowl. Combine bread crumbs, butter and coconut in another bowl. Spread half the blueberry mixture in prepared dish, top with half the apples and half the bread crumb mixture. Repeat layering, finishing with bread crumb mixture. Bake, uncovered, in 350°F oven about 1 hour or until browned.

Serves 6 to 8.

- Recipe can be made a day ahead.
- Storage: Covered, in refrigerator.
- Freeze: Not suitable.
- Microwave: Apples suitable.

HONEY DUMPLINGS

1¼ cups self-rising flour
2 tablespoons (¼ stick) butter, chopped
⅓ cup honey
⅓ cup milk

SAUCE
2 tablespoons (¼ stick) butter
¾ cup dark brown sugar, firmly packed
½ cup honey
1½ cups water

Sift flour into bowl, rub in butter. Stir in honey and milk, stir until just combined. Add level tablespoons of mixture to simmering sauce, cook, covered, about 25 minutes or until dumplings are puffed, golden and cooked through.

Sauce: Combine all ingredients in pan, stir over heat, without boiling, until sugar is dissolved, bring to boil, simmer, uncovered, 1 minute.

Serves 4.

- Recipe best made just before serving.
- Freeze: Not suitable.
- Microwave: Not suitable.

BELOW: Chocolate Whisky Fudge Cake.
RIGHT: From left: Honey Dumplings, Blueberry and Apple Brown Betty.

CREPES WITH FRUITY MACADAMIA SAUCE

1 cup all-purpose flour
2 teaspoons granulated sugar
4 eggs
3 tablespoons vegetable oil
1½ cups milk

FRUITY MACADAMIA SAUCE
1 tablespoon butter
¼ cup dark brown sugar
1¼ cups heavy cream
½ cup fresh orange juice
4 teaspoons fresh lemon juice
4 teaspoons custard powder
2 tablespoons water
¼ cup Grand Marnier
½ cup macadamias, toasted, halved
1½oz dried papaya, chopped
¼ cup dried currants
3 tablespoons chopped dried apples
3 tablespoons chopped dried pears

Sift flour and sugar into bowl, gradually stir in combined eggs, oil and milk; beat until smooth. Cover, stand 30 minutes.

Pour ¼ cup batter into heated greased heavy-based crepe pan, cook until lightly browned underneath. Turn crepe, brown other side. Repeat with remaining batter. You will need 12 crepes for this recipe. Fold crepes, serve topped with sauce.
Fruity Macadamia Sauce: Combine butter and sugar in pan, stir over heat, without boiling, until sugar is dissolved. Stir in cream, both juices and blended custard powder and water, stir over heat until sauce boils and thickens slightly. Add liqueur, nuts and fruit, stir over heat until well combined.

Serves 6.

▨ Recipe best made just before serving.
▨ Freeze: Not suitable.
▨ Microwave: Not suitable.

DATE BREAD AND BUTTER PUDDING

8 slices white bread
2 tablespoons (¼ stick) butter
1 cup (5½oz) chopped pitted dates
4 eggs
¼ cup granulated sugar
3 cups milk
1 teaspoon vanilla extract
½ teaspoon ground nutmeg

Grease 2 inch deep ovenproof dish (6 cup capacity). Remove crusts from bread. Butter bread, cut in half diagonally. Place half the bread, buttered-side-up, in prepared dish, sprinkle with dates, top with remaining bread. Whisk eggs, sugar, milk and extract in bowl. Pour milk mixture over bread, stand 10 minutes, sprinkle with nutmeg.

Place dish in roasting pan, pour in enough boiling water to come halfway up side of dish, bake, uncovered, in 325°F oven about 1¼ hours or until custard is set in the center.

Serves 6.

▨ Recipe best made just before serving.
▨ Freeze: Not suitable.
▨ Microwave: Not suitable.

SAGO APPLE PIE

3oz (¾ stick) butter
2oz lard
1 cup all-purpose flour
3 tablespoons water
6 large (about 2½lb) apples, peeled, cored, sliced
1½ teaspoons ground cinnamon
¾ cup dark brown sugar, firmly packed
3 tablespoons sago
1 egg white, lightly beaten
4 teaspoons sugar

Process butter, lard and flour until just combined, add water, process until mixture forms a ball; cover pastry, refrigerate 30 minutes.

Combine apples, cinnamon and brown sugar in bowl; mix well. Spoon half the apple mixture into ovenproof dish (6 cup capacity), sprinkle with sago, top with remaining apple mixture. Roll pastry between sheets of baking paper until large enough to cover pie dish, place over apples, trim edges; decorate with pastry scraps, if desired. Brush pastry with egg white, sprinkle with sugar. Cut 3 slits in top of pie. Bake in 350°F oven about 1½ hours or until pie is lightly browned.

Serves 6.

▨ Recipe can be made a day ahead.
▨ Storage: Covered in refrigerator.
▨ Freeze: Suitable.
▨ Microwave: Not suitable.

LEFT: From back: Date Bread and Butter Pudding, Crepes with Fruity Macadamia Sauce.
BELOW: Sago Apple Pie.

APRICOT STICKY TOFFEE PUDDING

1¼ cups (7oz) dried apricots, quartered
2 cups water
1 teaspoon baking soda
¼ cup (½ stick) butter
2 eggs
¾ cup dark brown sugar, firmly packed
½ cup granulated sugar
1½ cups self-rising flour
1 teaspoon vanilla extract

CARAMEL SAUCE
1 cup dark brown sugar, firmly packed
½ cup heavy cream
½ cup (1 stick) butter

Grease shallow 8 inch x 12 inch baking pan, line with baking paper.

Combine apricots and water in pan, simmer, uncovered, stirring occasionally, over low heat until thick and smooth. Transfer mixture to medium bowl, beat in remaining ingredients using wooden spoon. Pour mixture into prepared pan. Bake in 350°F oven about 25 minutes or until cooked through. Serve pudding with caramel sauce.

Caramel Sauce: Combine all ingredients in pan, stir over heat, without boiling, until sugar is dissolved. Bring to boil, simmer, uncovered, without stirring, 5 minutes.

Serves 6.

▓ Recipe can be made a day ahead.
▓ Storage: Airtight container.
▓ Freeze: Not suitable.
▓ Microwave: Not suitable.

FRUIT CRUMBLE WITH STREUSEL TOPPING

4 large (about 26oz) peaches
2 large (about 13oz) apples
1 lemon
2 tablespoons (¼ stick) butter
4 teaspoons fresh lemon juice
3 tablespoons dark brown sugar
⅓ cup water
¼ cup Grand Marnier
6 fresh dates, pitted
7oz fresh blueberries
½lb fresh strawberries
⅓ cup dark seedless raisins
4 teaspoons shredded coconut

STREUSEL TOPPING
⅓ cup shredded coconut, toasted
½ cup dark brown sugar,
   firmly packed
½ cup all-purpose flour
3oz (¾ stick) butter, melted

Peel peaches, cut in half; cut halves into thirds. Peel apples, cut in half; cut halves into quarters. Using a vegetable peeler, cut peel thinly from lemon, cut peel into thin strips.

Combine peel, butter, juice, sugar, water and liqueur in pan, stir over heat, without boiling, until sugar is dissolved; simmer, uncovered, without stirring, until mixture is reduced by one-third. Add peaches, apples, dates, blueberries, strawberries and raisins, simmer, covered, until apples are just tender.

Pour fruit mixture into ovenproof dish (6 cup capacity), sprinkle with topping and coconut. Bake in 375°F oven about 10 minutes or until topping is lightly browned and crisp.

Streusel Topping: Combine coconut, sugar and sifted flour in bowl, stir in butter; refrigerate 30 minutes or until firm.

Serves 6.

- Fruit and streusel topping can be prepared separately a day ahead.
- Storage: Covered, in refrigerator.
- Freeze: Streusel topping suitable.
- Microwave: Fruit suitable.

RHUBARB CUSTARD CAKE

½ cup (1 stick) butter
1 teaspoon vanilla extract
¾ cup granulated sugar
2 eggs
1½ cups self-rising flour
½ cup packaged ground almonds
½ cup milk

RHUBARB FILLING
7oz rhubarb, chopped
3 tablespoons granulated sugar
2 teaspoons water

CUSTARD
½ cup milk
3 tablespoons granulated sugar
1 teaspoon vanilla extract
3 tablespoons custard powder
¼ cup milk, extra

Grease deep 9 inch round baking pan, cover base with paper; grease paper. Cream butter, extract and sugar in small bowl with electric mixer until light and fluffy; beat in eggs 1 at a time. Transfer mixture to large bowl, stir in sifted flour, nuts and milk.

Spread half the cake mixture into prepared pan. Drop teaspoons of rhubarb filling and custard alternately on to cake mixture. Top with remaining cake mixture, spread gently. Bake in 350°F oven about 1 hour or until browned and cooked through. Stand cake in pan 5 minutes before turning onto wire rack. Serve cake warm or cold.

Rhubarb Filling: Combine rhubarb, sugar and water in pan, simmer, covered, until rhubarb is soft. Simmer, stirring, until thick; cool.

Custard: Combine milk, sugar and extract in pan, stir in blended custard powder and extra milk. Stir over heat until mixture boils and thickens. Pour into bowl, cover surface with plastic wrap; cool.

Serves 6.

- Cake can be made 3 days ahead.
- Storage: Airtight container.
- Freeze: Suitable.
- Microwave: Rhubarb filling and custard suitable.

LEFT: Apricot Sticky Toffee Pudding.
BELOW LEFT: Fruit Crumble with Streusel Topping.
BELOW: Rhubarb Custard Cake.

RICH CHOCOLATE AND HAZELNUT PUDDING

3oz (¾ stick) butter
¼ cup granulated sugar
3 tablespoons brandy
4 eggs, separated
¼lb semisweet chocolate, melted
½ cup all-purpose flour
¾ cup ground hazelnuts
½ cup fresh bread crumbs
¼ cup granulated sugar, extra

CHOCOLATE SAUCE
7oz bittersweet chocolate
3 tablespoons butter
3 tablespoons brandy
¾ cup heavy cream

Grease pudding steamer (6 cup capacity). Beat butter, sugar and brandy in small bowl with electric mixer until light and fluffy. Stir in egg yolks and cooled chocolate. Transfer mixture to large bowl, fold in sifted flour, nuts and bread crumbs.

Beat egg whites in small bowl with electric mixer until soft peaks form, gradually add extra sugar; beat until dissolved. Fold egg whites into chocolate mixture in 2 batches. Pour into prepared steamer, cover with greased paper, then foil, secure with kitchen string or lid. Place steamer in large pan with enough boiling water to come halfway up side of steamer. Boil, covered, about 1¾ hours or until pudding is firm. Replenish water as necessary. Stand pudding 5 minutes before turning out. Serve hot pudding with chocolate sauce.

Chocolate Sauce: Melt chocolate over hot water, add butter and brandy, stir until butter is melted; stir in cream.

Serves 6.

- Pudding can be made a day ahead.
- Storage: Covered, in refrigerator.
- Freeze: Pudding suitable.
- Microwave: Chocolate sauce suitable.

RICOTTA PIE WITH COCONUT APRICOT TOPPING

7oz amaretti cookies
½ cup packaged ground almonds
1 cup (2½oz) dried apples, finely chopped
½ cup (1 stick) butter, melted

FILLING
¾lb ricotta cheese
½ cup sour cream
¼ cup granulated sugar
2 eggs
¼ cup shredded coconut
2 teaspoons grated orange zest

COCONUT APRICOT TOPPING
1 teaspoon vegetable oil
1 cup (2½oz) shredded coconut
½ cup dried apricots, finely chopped
1 cup confectioners' sugar
3 tablespoons sour cream

Grease 9 inch flan pan. Crush or process cookies until fine. Combine cookie crumbs, almonds, apples and butter in bowl; mix well. Press mixture firmly over base and side of prepared pan. Bake in 350°F oven about 10 minutes or until browned; cool.

Pour filling into prepared case, bake in 300°F oven about 40 minutes or until filling is firm; cool. Spread evenly with coconut apricot topping.
Filling: Beat cheese, cream, sugar and eggs in bowl until smooth, stir in coconut and zest; mix well.
Coconut Apricot Topping: Heat oil in pan, add coconut, cook, stirring, until coconut is lightly browned. Stir in remaining ingredients, stir until combined; cool 5 minutes before using.

Serves 6 to 8.

- Recipe can be made a day ahead.
- Storage: Covered, in refrigerator.
- Freeze: Not suitable.
- Microwave: Not suitable.

ORANGE AND PEAR CREME CARAMEL

½ cup granulated sugar
½ cup water
¼ cup Cointreau or Curacao

CUSTARD
½ cup granulated sugar
1 cup water
2 medium (about 10oz) pears, chopped
6 eggs
⅓ cup granulated sugar, extra
1 cup milk
1¼ cups heavy cream
2 teaspoons grated orange zest

Combine sugar, water and liqueur in heavy-based pan, stir over heat, without boiling, until sugar is dissolved. Boil, un-covered, without stirring, until mixture turns golden brown. Pour over base of deep 8 inch round baking pan. When caramel is set, pour over custard mixture.

Place pan in roasting pan with enough boiling water to come halfway up side of baking pan. Bake in 325°F oven about 45 minutes or until custard is just set.

Remove pan from water, cool, cover, refrigerate overnight. Turn out creme caramel just before serving.
Custard: Combine sugar and water in pan, stir over heat, without boiling, until sugar is dissolved. Boil, uncovered, without stirring, 2 minutes. Add pears, simmer, covered, until pears are tender. Drain pears, discard syrup. Blend or process pears until smooth; push through fine sieve. Lightly whisk eggs in large bowl with extra sugar and pear puree until combined. Combine milk, cream and zest in pan, bring to boil, allow bubbles to sub-side, gradually whisk into egg mixture.

Serves 6 to 8.

- Recipe best made a day ahead, will keep for 2 days.
- Storage: Covered, in refrigerator.
- Freeze: Not suitable.
- Microwave: Not suitable.

LEFT: From back: Rich Chocolate and Hazelnut Pudding, Ricotta Pie with Coconut Apricot Topping.
RIGHT: Orange and Pear Creme Caramel.

Baking

Golden-crusted bread and rolls fresh from the oven are a special pleasure. Remember to knead doughs well, and don't over-flour the bench as this can upset the balance of ingredients. Tap breads with a finger to test for doneness; if they sound hollow, they are cooked. Cover breads with foil if over-browning. As an added treat, we've also made hot biscuits, muffins and griddle cakes, all very quick.

SAFFRON AND FENNEL ROLLS

1½ packages (⅓oz) active dry yeast
1 teaspoon sugar
3 tablespoons warm water
4 cups (20oz) all-purpose flour
2 teaspoons salt
⅛ teaspoon ground saffron
3 tablespoons butter, melted
2 eggs, lightly beaten
1 cup milk
2 tablespoons fennel seeds
1 teaspoon vegetable oil

Grease and flour baking sheet. Combine yeast, sugar and water in small bowl, cover, stand about 10 minutes or until mixture is frothy. Sift flour, salt and saffron into large bowl, stir in yeast mixture, then combined butter, eggs, milk and seeds; mix to a firm dough. Turn dough onto lightly floured surface, knead about 5 minutes or until smooth and elastic. Return dough to large greased bowl, cover, stand in warm place about 1½ hours or until dough is doubled in size.

Turn dough onto floured surface, knead until smooth. Roll dough into a 16 inch sausage, cut into 2 inch lengths, place on prepared baking sheet. Cover with damp cloth, stand in warm place about 40 minutes or until rolls have doubled in size. Brush rolls lightly with oil, bake in 350°F oven about 1 hour or until browned and sound hollow when tapped.

Makes 8.

- Recipe best made on day of serving.
- Storage: Airtight container.
- Freeze: Suitable.
- Microwave: Not suitable.

WHEATMEAL ROLLS

1¼ cups whole-wheat self-rising flour
1¼ cups self-rising flour
2 teaspoons sugar
1 teaspoon salt
¼ cup (½ stick) butter, chopped
¼ cup coarse wheatmeal
¾ cup milk, approximately
1 egg yolk
4 teaspoons milk, extra

TOPPINGS
½ teaspoon whole-wheat flour
½ teaspoon fine sea salt
½ teaspoon dried mixed herbs
½ teaspoon poppy seeds
½ teaspoon sesame seeds
½ teaspoon caraway seeds

Sift flours, sugar and salt into bowl, rub in butter. Stir in wheatmeal and enough milk to make a soft dough. Knead dough gently on floured surface until smooth. Divide mixture into 12 portions. Knead each portion until smooth.

Place 1 roll in center and 5 rolls, almost touching, around outside on 2 lightly greased baking sheets. Brush rolls with combined egg yolk and extra milk, sprinkle rolls with ¼ teaspoon of each different topping, not repeating a topping on the same baking sheet. Bake rolls in 375°F oven about 20 minutes or until browned and sound hollow when tapped.

Makes 12.

- Recipe best made on day of serving.
- Storage: Airtight container.
- Freeze: Suitable.
- Microwave: Not suitable.

RIGHT: From left: Wheatmeal Rolls, Saffron and Fennel Rolls.

BASIC BISCUITS

2 cups self-rising flour
2 teaspoons sugar
1 tablespoon butter
1 cup milk, approximately

Grease 8 inch round baking pan. Sift flour and sugar into bowl, rub in butter, stir in enough milk to mix to a soft sticky dough. Turn dough onto floured surface, knead lightly until smooth. Press dough out to about 1 inch thickness, cut into 2 inch rounds. Place biscuits into prepared pan, brush with a little extra milk. Bake in 450°F oven about 15 minutes.

VARIATIONS

Currant and Apricot: Add 3 tablespoons dried currants and ¼ cup finely chopped dried apricots to dry ingredients.
Date and Golden Raisin: Add ¼ cup finely chopped dried dates and ¼ cup chopped golden raisins to dry ingredients.
Herb: Add 2 tablespoons chopped fresh parsley, 2 tablespoons chopped fresh chives, 2 teaspoons chopped fresh dill and 4 teaspoons chopped fresh basil to dry ingredients.
Ham and Cheese: Add ⅓ cup grated Parmesan cheese, ½ cup grated cheddar cheese and 4 slices finely chopped cooked ham to dry ingredients.

Makes about 12.

- Recipe best made on day of serving.
- Storage: Airtight container.
- Freeze: Suitable.
- Microwave: Not suitable.

IRISH SODA AND RAISIN BREAD

4½ cups (22oz) all-purpose flour
1½ teaspoons baking soda
1 teaspoon cream of tartar
1 teaspoon salt
¾ cup granulated sugar
3oz (¾ stick) butter, melted
⅓ cup chopped dark seedless raisins
1¾ cups buttermilk

Grease and flour 5½ inch x 8½ inch loaf pan. Sift flour, soda, cream of tartar, salt and sugar into large bowl, stir in butter, raisins and buttermilk; mix to a firm dough. Turn dough onto lightly floured surface, knead about 5 minutes or until dough is smooth and elastic; shape dough to fit prepared pan. Slash top of loaf diagonally. Bake in 325°F oven about 1½ hours or until bread is browned and sounds hollow when tapped.

Makes 1.

- Recipe best made on day of serving.
- Storage: Airtight container.
- Freeze: Suitable.
- Microwave: Not suitable.

BELOW: Clockwise from top left: Basic Biscuits, Herb Biscuits, Currant and Apricot Biscuits, Ham and Cheese Biscuits, Date and Golden Raisin Biscuits.
RIGHT: From left: Irish Soda and Raisin Bread, Savory Brioche Rolls.

SAVORY BRIOCHE ROLLS

1 package (¼oz) active dry yeast
⅔ cup warm water
4 teaspoons sugar
4 cups (20oz) all-purpose flour
4 eggs, lightly beaten
¾ cup (1½ sticks) butter, chopped
1 egg yolk
3 tablespoons heavy cream
fine sea salt

FILLING
1 tablespoon butter
1 small onion, finely chopped
2 cloves garlic, minced
7oz csabai salami, chopped
4 teaspoons chopped fresh basil

Combine yeast, water and 1 teaspoon of the sugar in a small bowl, cover, stand in a warm place about 10 minutes or until mixture is frothy.

Sift flour and remaining sugar into large bowl, stir in yeast mixture and eggs; mix to a firm dough. Turn dough onto floured surface, knead about 10 minutes or until smooth. Gradually knead in pieces of butter, knead until smooth. Place dough into large greased bowl, cover, stand in warm place about 1 hour or until dough is doubled in size.

Divide dough and filling into 12 portions. Roll a portion of the dough into 6 inch circle. Place a portion of filling in center of dough. Pinch edges together to enclose filling. Repeat with remaining dough and filling. Place rolls seam-side-down on greased baking sheet, stand, uncovered, in warm place about 15 minutes or until rolls are doubled in size.

Cut 3 slits along top of each roll, brush with combined egg yolk and cream, sprinkle with salt. Bake in 350°F oven about 40 minutes or until rolls are browned and sound hollow when tapped.
Filling: Heat butter in pan, add onion and garlic, cook, stirring, until onion is soft; cool. Transfer mixture to bowl; stir in csabai and basil.

Makes 12.

- Recipe best made on day of serving.
- Storage: Airtight container.
- Freeze: Suitable.
- Microwave: Not suitable.

POPPY SEED ROLLS

1 package (¼oz) active dry yeast
1 teaspoon sugar
½ cup warm water
3⅓ cups (1lb) all-purpose flour
1 teaspoon salt
3 tablespoons poppy seeds
1 cup warm water, extra
1 egg, lightly beaten
1 teaspoon poppy seeds, extra

Cream yeast with sugar in small bowl; stir in water, cover, stand in warm place about 10 minutes or until mixture is frothy. Sift flour and salt into large bowl, stir in poppy seeds. Stir in yeast mixture and extra water. Cover, stand in warm place about 1 hour or until dough is doubled in size.

Turn dough onto floured surface, knead about 5 minutes or until smooth and elastic. Shape dough into 12 oval rolls, brush with egg, sprinkle with extra poppy seeds. Make 3 slits on top of rolls. Place rolls on greased baking sheet, stand, uncovered, in warm place about 20 minutes or until dough is well risen. Bake in 375°F oven about 20 minutes or until rolls are browned; cool on wire rack.

Makes 12.

- Rolls can be made a day ahead.
- Storage: Airtight container.
- Freeze: Suitable.
- Microwave: Not suitable.

CORN BREAD

1 package (¼oz) active dry yeast
½ cup warm water
½ cup warm milk
2 cups all-purpose flour
½ cup cornmeal
½ teaspoon salt
2 teaspoons cornmeal, extra

Mix yeast with water in bowl; stir in milk. Sift flour into large bowl, stir in cornmeal and salt. Stir in yeast mixture; mix to a firm dough. Knead dough on floured surface about 10 minutes or until dough is smooth and elastic. Place dough into greased bowl; cover, stand in warm place about 1 hour or until doubled in size.

Turn dough onto floured surface, knead further 5 minutes. Shape dough into 5 inch round, place on lightly greased baking sheet. Cut slashes in top of bread to form a cross. Stand, covered, in warm place 20 minutes, sprinkle with extra cornmeal. Bake in 375°F oven about 20 minutes or until bread sounds hollow when tapped.

Makes 1.

- Recipe best made on day of serving.
- Storage: Airtight container.
- Freeze: Suitable.
- Microwave: Not suitable.

FLOWER POT BREAD

It is necessary to season flower pots before use. Brush pots with vegetable oil, place on baking sheet, bake in 375°F oven about 3 hours, brushing occasionally with oil. Flower pot bread can also be made in 6 x 4 inch terracotta pots; cooking time will be about 25 minutes.

2 packages (½oz) active dry yeast
2 teaspoons sugar
½ cup warm milk
6½ cups (2lb) all-purpose flour
2 teaspoons salt
2½ cups warm milk, extra
3 tablespoons vegetable oil
1 egg yolk
1 teaspoon cold milk
4 teaspoons wheatgerm

Combine yeast, sugar and warm milk in small bowl, cover, stand in warm place about 10 minutes or until mixture is frothy.

Sift flour and salt into large bowl, stir in yeast mixture, extra warm milk and oil; mix to a soft dough. Turn dough onto floured surface, knead about 3 minutes or until dough is smooth and elastic. Place dough into large greased bowl, cover, stand in warm place about 40 minutes or until dough is doubled in size.

Turn dough onto lightly floured surface, knead until smooth. Grease 3 x 5½ inch terracotta pots. Cover base of pots with paper. Divide dough into 3 portions, shape each portion to fill prepared pots.

Stand pots in warm place about 40 minutes or until dough is risen to top of pots. Brush dough with combined egg and cold milk, sprinkle with wheatgerm. Bake in 375°F oven about 35 minutes or until bread is well browned and sounds hollow when tapped. Stand bread in pots for about 5 minutes before turning onto wire rack to cool.

Makes 3.

- Recipe best made on day of serving.
- Storage: Airtight container.
- Freeze: Suitable.
- Microwave: Not suitable.

RIGHT: Clockwise from top left: Flower Pot Bread, Poppy Seed Rolls, Corn Bread.

GRANOLA LOAF

1 package (¼oz) active dry yeast
1 teaspoon sugar
¼ cup warm water
1 cup boiling water
⅓ cup dark brown sugar
1½ cups (6½oz) toasted granola
½ cup chopped dried apricots
½ cup golden raisins
1 cup whole-wheat flour
2 cups all-purpose flour
1 teaspoon mixed spice
¼ cup wheatgerm
1 egg, lightly beaten
½ cup milk

GLAZE
½ teaspoon sugar
½ teaspoon unflavored gelatin
2 teaspoons water

Grease 5½ inch x 8½ inch loaf pan. Combine yeast with sugar in small bowl, stir in warm water, cover, stand in warm place about 10 minutes or until frothy. Combine boiling water, brown sugar, granola, apricots and golden raisins in bowl; cover, stand until liquid is absorbed.

Sift flours and spice into bowl; stir in yeast mixture, granola mixture, wheat-germ, egg and milk; mix to a soft dough. Knead dough on floured surface about 10 minutes or until smooth and elastic. Transfer dough to large greased bowl, cover, stand in warm place about 1 hour or until dough is doubled in size. Turn dough onto floured surface, knead 5 minutes. Shape dough to fit into prepared pan; cover, stand in warm place about 45 minutes or until almost doubled in size. Bake in 375°F oven 15 minutes; reduce heat to 350°F, bake further 1 hour or until bread sounds hollow when tapped. Remove bread from pan; brush evenly with hot glaze.

Glaze: Sprinkle sugar and gelatin over water in cup, stand in small pan of simmering water, stir until dissolved.

Makes 1.

- Recipe best made on day of serving.
- Storage: Airtight container.
- Freeze: Suitable.
- Microwave: Glaze suitable.

BELOW: From left: Cottage Cheese and Dill Bread, Granola Loaf.

COTTAGE CHEESE AND DILL BREAD

1 package (¼oz) active dry yeast
½ cup warm water
3 tablespoons honey
4 cups (20oz) all-purpose flour
1 teaspoon salt
1 small red onion, finely chopped
¼ cup chopped fresh dill
8oz carton cottage cheese
1 egg, lightly beaten
½ cup milk
¼ cup olive oil
1 egg yolk
4 teaspoons milk, extra

Combine yeast, water and honey in bowl, cover, stand in warm place about 10 minutes or until frothy. Sift flour and salt into bowl; stir in yeast mixture, onion, dill, cheese, egg, milk and oil; mix to a soft dough. Knead dough on floured surface about 10 minutes or until smooth and elastic. Place dough in large greased bowl, cover, stand in warm place about 1 hour or until doubled in size.

Turn dough onto floured surface, knead 5 minutes. Divide dough in half, shape each half into a 20 inch sausage. Shape into rings about 8 inches in diameter; join

ends. Place bread onto greased baking sheets, stand, uncovered, in warm place about 30 minutes or until almost doubled in size. Brush bread with combined egg yolk and extra milk, bake in 375°F oven 15 minutes, reduce heat to 350°F, bake further 15 minutes or until browned and cooked through.

Makes 2.

- Recipe best made on day of serving.
- Storage: Airtight container.
- Freeze: Suitable.
- Microwave: Not suitable.

BASIC MUFFINS

2 cups self-rising flour
1 cup all-purpose flour
1 teaspoon baking soda
1 cup dark brown sugar,
   firmly packed
2 eggs, lightly beaten
1½ cups milk
¾ cup vegetable oil

TOPPING
¼ cup dark brown sugar
¼ cup all-purpose flour
3 tablespoons butter, chopped

Grease 16 x ⅓ cup muffin tins. Sift dry ingredients into bowl, stir in sugar, then combined eggs, milk and oil; do not over-mix, batter should be lumpy. Add ingredients for each variation, following methods given. Bake in 375°F oven about 20 minutes or until browned and firm. Stand 2 minutes, remove from tins; cool on wire rack.
Topping: Combine sugar and flour in bowl; rub in butter.

MUFFIN VARIATIONS

APPLE CINNAMON

2 teaspoons ground cinnamon
1 cup finely chopped apple
½ cup finely chopped apple, extra

Sift cinnamon with dry ingredients, stir in apple. Spoon into prepared muffin tins. Sprinkle muffins with extra apple and topping mixture.

BELOW: From left in basket: Blueberry Muffins, Apple Cinnamon Muffins, Banana Walnut Muffins.

BLUEBERRY

7oz fresh blueberries

Spoon half the basic muffin mixture into prepared tins, sprinkle with ¾ cup blueberries, spoon over remaining mixture. Sprinkle with remaining blueberries and topping mixture.

BANANA WALNUT

1 cup mashed over-ripe bananas
½ cup chopped walnuts
½ cup chopped walnuts, extra

Stir bananas and walnuts into basic mixture. Spoon into prepared muffin tins. Sprinkle muffins with extra walnuts and topping mixture.

Makes 16.

- Recipe can be made a day ahead.
- Storage: Airtight container.
- Freeze: Suitable.
- Microwave: Not suitable.

OLIVE BREAD

1 package (¼oz) active dry yeast
1 teaspoon sugar
1 cup warm buttermilk
3 tablespoons warm water
1 egg, lightly beaten
¼ cup olive oil
3¼ cups (1lb) all-purpose flour
¼ cup black olive paste
1 egg, lightly beaten, extra

Grease 4½ inch x 9 inch loaf pan. Combine yeast, sugar, buttermilk and water in bowl, cover, stand in warm place about 15 minutes or until mixture is frothy. Stir in egg and oil.

Sift flour into large bowl, stir in yeast mixture, mix to a soft dough. Turn dough onto floured surface, knead until smooth. Place dough into lightly oiled bowl, cover, stand in warm place about 1 hour or until dough is doubled in size.

Knead dough on lightly floured surface until smooth. Roll dough to a rectangle about 8 inches x 10½ inches. Spread dough with olive paste, roll up tightly from short side. Place in prepared pan, cover, stand in warm place about 40 minutes or until dough is almost doubled in size. Brush loaf with extra egg, bake in 375°F oven 10 minutes, reduce heat to 350°F, bake further 25 minutes or until loaf sounds hollow when tapped.

Makes 1.

- Recipe best made on day of serving.
- Storage: Airtight container.
- Freeze: Suitable.
- Microwave: Not suitable.

TOASTED SUNFLOWER SEED BREAD

¾ cup sunflower seeds
2 teaspoons light soy sauce
½ cup warm water
1 package (¼oz) active dry yeast
2 teaspoons dark brown sugar
2 cups whole-wheat flour
1 cup all-purpose flour
1 chicken bouillon cube
½ cup water, extra
½ cup milk
1 egg yolk
2 teaspoons milk, extra

Add seeds to dry pan, shake over heat until lightly browned, add sauce; cool. Reserve ¼ cup seeds, process the remaining seeds until coarsely ground.

Grease 5½ inch x 8½ inch loaf pan. Place 3 tablespoons ground seeds in pan, shake to coat pan.

Combine warm water, yeast and sugar in small bowl, cover, stand in warm place about 10 minutes or until frothy.

Sift flours into bowl, stir in remaining ground seeds, reserved seeds, yeast mixture, crumbled bouillon cube, extra water and milk; mix to a soft dough. Knead dough on floured surface 10 minutes or until smooth. Place dough into large greased bowl, stand in warm place about 1 hour or until dough is doubled in size.

Turn dough onto floured surface, knead about 5 minutes or until smooth. Shape dough to fit prepared pan, stand in warm place about 45 minutes or until doubled in size. Brush dough evenly with combined egg yolk and extra milk. Bake in 375°F oven about 45 minutes or until browned and cooked through.

Makes 1.

- Recipe best made on day of serving.
- Storage: Airtight container.
- Freeze: Suitable.
- Microwave: Not suitable.

CINNAMON RAISIN BREAD

1 cup (3oz) old fashioned oats
¾ cup warm milk
1 cup (5½oz) dark seedless raisins
¾ cup (1½ sticks) unsalted butter,
  softened
1 cup dark brown sugar,
  firmly packed
3 eggs
½ cup sour cream
2 teaspoons vanilla extract
1½ cups whole-wheat flour
¾ cup all-purpose flour
½ cup self-rising flour
1 teaspoon baking soda
4 teaspoons ground cinnamon
½ teaspoon ground nutmeg

TOPPING
½ cup old fashioned oats
2 teaspoons ground cinnamon
3 tablespoons dark brown sugar
1 tablespoon butter

Grease 2 x 5½ inch x 8½ inch loaf pans. Combine oats, milk and raisins in bowl, cover, stand 1 hour.

Beat butter and sugar in small bowl with electric mixer until smooth, add eggs 1 at a time, beat well after each addition. Beat in sour cream and extract. Transfer mixture to large bowl, stir in oat mixture. Sift dry ingredients together; stir into oat mixture in 3 batches. The dough will be sticky.

Divide mixture between prepared pans, sprinkle with topping. Bake in 350°F oven about 50 minutes or until browned. Stand 15 minutes before turning onto wire rack to cool.
Topping: Combine oats, cinnamon and sugar in bowl, rub in butter.

Makes 2.

- Recipe best made on day of serving.
- Storage: Airtight container.
- Freeze: Suitable.
- Microwave: Not suitable.

LEFT: From left: Toasted Sunflower Seed Bread, Olive Bread, Cinnamon Raisin Bread.
ABOVE: Golden Spicy Griddle Cakes.

GOLDEN SPICY GRIDDLE CAKES

1 cup self-rising flour
¼ cup dark brown sugar
⅛ teaspoon baking soda
1 teaspoon ground gingerroot
½ teaspoon mixed spice
½ teaspoon ground cinnamon
⅛ teaspoon ground cloves
1 egg, lightly beaten
4 teaspoons honey
¾ cup milk, approximately

Sift dry ingredients into bowl. Make well in center, gradually stir in egg, honey and enough milk to give a creamy pouring consistency; stir until smooth. (Or, blend or process all ingredients until smooth.)

Drop rounded tablespoons of mixture about 2 inches apart into heated greased griddle. When bubbles appear, turn cakes, cook until lightly browned on other side. Serve warm with butter and extra honey, if desired.

Makes about 15.

- Recipe best made just before serving.
- Freeze: Suitable.
- Microwave: Not suitable.

POTATO AND ROSEMARY FOCACCIA

2 medium (about 10oz) potatoes
2 packages (¹/₂oz) active dry yeast
¹/₂ cup warm water
4 cups (20oz) all-purpose flour
1 teaspoon salt
¹/₂ cup warm milk
2 medium (about 10oz) potatoes, extra
3 cloves garlic, sliced
3 tablespoons fresh rosemary leaves
¹/₃ cup olive oil

Lightly grease 10¹/₂ inch x 13 inch jelly-roll pan. Boil, steam or microwave potatoes until tender, drain; mash, cool.

Cream yeast with a little of the water in small bowl, stand in a warm place about 10 minutes or until mixture is frothy.

Sift flour and salt into large bowl, rub in mashed potato. Stir in yeast mixture, remaining water and milk, mix to a firm dough. Turn dough onto lightly floured surface, knead about 5 minutes or until dough is smooth and elastic. Return dough to large greased bowl, cover, stand in warm place about 2 hours or until dough is doubled in size.

Turn dough onto floured surface, knead until smooth, press dough into prepared pan, cover, stand in warm place about 1 hour or until dough is doubled in size.

Peel and thinly slice extra potatoes, arrange slices overlapping on top of dough. Sprinkle with garlic and rosemary; brush with oil. Bake in 350°F oven about 1 hour or until potatoes are soft. Cool focaccia in pan.

Serves 4 to 6.

- Recipe best made on day of serving.
- Freeze: Not suitable.
- Microwave: Potatoes suitable.

INDIVIDUAL RUM BABAS

1 package (¹/₄oz) active dry yeast
4 teaspoons granulated sugar
¹/₄ cup warm milk
1 cup all-purpose flour
4 teaspoons granulated sugar, extra
2 eggs, lightly beaten
¹/₄ cup (¹/₂ stick) butter, melted
¹/₃ cup golden raisins

SYRUP
1 cup granulated sugar
1¹/₂ cups water
1 teaspoon grated orange zest
¹/₄ cup dark rum

Lightly grease 6 brioche pans (¹/₃ cup capacity). Combine yeast, sugar and milk in small bowl, cover, stand in warm place about 10 minutes or until mixture is frothy.

Sift flour and extra sugar into large bowl, stir in yeast mixture, eggs and cooled butter, beat about 3 minutes with wooden spoon or until batter is smooth.

Place batter in large greased bowl, cover, stand in warm place about 40 minutes or until batter is doubled in size.

Add raisins, stir mixture until flattened. Divide batter between prepared pans, stand, uncovered, until batter rises to top of pans. Bake in 375°F oven about 12 minutes or until babas are cooked through. Turn onto wire rack over tray. Pour hot syrup over warm babas, place on serving plate, pour syrup from tray over babas until all syrup is absorbed; cool.

Syrup: Combine sugar, water, zest and rum in pan. Stir over heat, without boiling, until sugar is dissolved, boil, uncovered, without stirring, 2 minutes.

Serves 6.

- Recipe best made on day of serving.
- Storage: Airtight container.
- Freeze: Not suitable.
- Microwave: Not suitable.

TEACAKE WITH CARAMEL FROSTING

1 package (¼oz) active dry yeast
3½ cups (17½oz) all-purpose flour
3 tablespoons sugar
1 cup warm milk
3oz (¾ stick) butter, melted
1 egg, lightly beaten

FILLING
½ cup golden raisins
¼ cup dried currants
2 tablespoons mixed peel
½ teaspoon ground cinnamon
½ teaspoon mixed spice
¼ cup dark brown sugar
2 tablespoons (¼ stick) butter, melted

GLAZE
4 teaspoons water
1 teaspoon unflavored gelatin
4 teaspoons sugar

CARAMEL FROSTING
1 tablespoon butter
⅓ cup dark brown sugar
3 teaspoons water
½ cup confectioners' sugar

Combine yeast, 1 teaspoon of the flour and 1 teaspoon of the sugar and milk in small bowl, cover, stand in warm place about 10 minutes or until frothy.

Sift remaining flour into bowl, stir in remaining sugar. Stir in yeast mixture, butter and egg; mix well. Turn dough onto floured surface, knead about 5 minutes or until smooth. Return dough to greased bowl, cover, stand in warm place about 40 minutes or until doubled in size.

Turn dough onto lightly floured surface, knead about 5 minutes or until smooth.

Roll dough into 8½ inch x 11 inch rectangle, place on greased baking sheet. Sprinkle filling down center third of the dough. Make about 15 cuts in the dough at ¾ inch intervals on either side of the filling. Fold strips of dough across filling in a criss-cross pattern. Brush with a little extra milk, stand, uncovered, in warm place until increased in size by half.

Bake in 400°F oven 10 minutes, reduce heat to 350°F, bake further 15 minutes. Remove from oven, brush with glaze; cool. Drizzle with caramel frosting.

Filling: Combine all ingredients in bowl; mix well.

Glaze: Combine water, unflavored gelatin and sugar in cup, stand in small pan of simmering water, stir until dissolved.

Caramel Frosting: Combine butter, sugar and water in pan, stir over heat, without boiling, until sugar is dissolved. Remove from heat, stir in sifted confectioners' sugar. Use while warm.

Serves 6 to 8.

- Recipe best made on day of serving.
- Storage: Airtight container.
- Freeze: Suitable.
- Microwave: Glaze suitable.

FAR LEFT: Potato and Rosemary Focaccia.
LEFT: Individual Rum Babas.
BELOW: Teacake with Caramel Frosting.

CREAM BUNS

1 package (¼oz) active dry yeast
4 cups (20oz) all-purpose flour
¼ cup granulated sugar
½ cup warm milk
½ teaspoon mixed spice
3oz (¾ stick) butter, chopped
⅓ cup golden raisins
1 cup warm water
4 teaspoons milk, extra
2 tablespoons raspberry preserves

GLAZE
4 teaspoons granulated sugar
1 teaspoon unflavored gelatin
4 teaspoons water

WASHED MOCK CREAM
1 cup (2 sticks) butter
2 teaspoons vanilla extract
1 cup granulated sugar

Combine yeast, 1 teaspoon of the flour, 1 teaspoon of the sugar and warm milk in small bowl, cover, stand in warm place about 10 minutes or until mixture is frothy. Sift remaining flour and spice into large bowl, stir in remaining sugar. Rub in butter, stir in raisins. Stir in yeast mixture and water, mix to a soft dough.

Turn dough onto floured surface, knead about 5 minutes or until dough is smooth and elastic. Return dough to large greased bowl, cover, stand in warm place about 40 minutes or until dough is doubled in size.

Turn dough onto floured surface, knead until smooth. Divide dough into 12 portions. Knead each portion into a ball, place on greased baking sheets, stand, uncovered, in warm place about 15 minutes or until dough is well risen. Brush dough evenly with extra milk, bake in 400°F oven about 10 minutes, reduce heat to 350°F, bake further 10 minutes or until cooked.

Brush buns with glaze while hot, cool on wire racks. Split cold buns, fill with some of the preserves, top with mock cream, then some more preserves Dust tops lightly with sifted confectioners' sugar, if desired.

Glaze: Sprinkle sugar and gelatin over water in cup, stand in small pan of simmering water, stir until dissolved.

Washed Mock Cream: Cream butter, extract and sugar in small bowl with electric mixer until light and fluffy. Remove bowl from mixer, cover butter mixture with cold water, swirl around bowl for 1 minute, pour off water. Repeat washing and beating until mixture is white in color and all the sugar dissolved. You will need to do this about 6 times.

Makes 12.

- Recipe best made on day of serving.
- Storage: Airtight container.
- Freeze: Unfilled buns suitable.
- Microwave: Glaze suitable.

BELOW: Cream Buns.

Glossary

Here are some terms, names and alternatives to help everyone understand and use our recipes perfectly.

ALCOHOL: is optional, but gives a particular flavor. Use fruit juice or water instead to make up the liquid content required in our recipes.

ALMONDS
Ground: we used packaged commercially ground nuts unless otherwise specified.
Sliced: almonds cut into thin slices.
Slivered: almonds cut lengthways.
AMARETTI COOKIES: small Italian-style macaroons based on ground almonds.
BACON SLICES: we used thick slices of bacon.

BEANS
Borlotti: pale brown beans with burgundy colored markings. A smooth texture with a ham-like flavor when cooked. Require soaking. See picture on page 124.
Haricot: small, white, oval beans with a smooth texture and bland flavor. Require soaking. See picture on page 124.
Lima: kidney-shaped beans; pale green or cream in color. Require soaking. See picture on page 124.
BEAN SPROUTS: we used alfalfa and mung bean sprouts; either can be used.

BEEF
Boneless beef chuck: is cut from the neck of the animal. Recommended for long cooking.
Fresh corned beef: is cut from the outside portion of the upper leg and cured.
Ground beef: we used lean ground beef.
BONED: ask your butcher to remove the bone in meat cuts as specified.

BREAD CRUMBS
Fresh: use 1 or 2 day old white bread made into crumbs by grating, blending or processing.
Packaged unseasoned: use fine packaged unseasoned bread crumbs.
BROTH: 1 cup broth is the equivalent of 1 cup water plus 1 crumbled bouillon cube (or 1 teaspoon bouillon powder). If you prefer to make fresh broth, see recipes on page 125.
BUTTER: use salted or unsalted.
BUTTERFLIED: ask your butcher to remove bone and "butterfly" the meat so that it lies flat.
CALVADOS: apple-flavored brandy.

CHEESE
Cheddar: use a firm, good-tasting cheddar.
Cottage: we used low-fat cottage cheese.
Cream: unripened, smooth spreadable cheese.

Gorgonzola: a type of blue vein cheese, native to Italy.
Gruyere: a hard yellow cheese with holes the size of peas and a strong fruity flavor.
Mascarpone: a fresh, unripened, smooth, triple cream cheese with a rich, sweet taste; slightly acidic.
Mozzarella: a fresh, semi-soft cheese with a delicate, clean, fresh curd taste; has a low melting point and stringy texture when it is heated.
Parmesan: sharp-tasting cheese used as a flavor accent. We prefer to use fresh Parmesan cheese, although it is available already finely grated.
Ricotta: a fresh, unripened light curd cheese.
Smoked: use a firm smoked cheese.
Swiss: a light yellow-colored cheese with holes varying in size from that of a hazelnut to a cherry; a smooth mellow texture and a nut-like flavor.
CHICORY: a curly leafed vegetable, mainly used in salads.
CHILIES: are available in many different types and sizes. The small ones (birds' eye or bird peppers) are the hottest. Use tight rubber gloves when chopping fresh chilies as they can burn your skin.
Flakes, dried: available at Asian food stores.
CILANTRO: also known as Chinese parsley. A strongly flavored herb, use it sparingly until accustomed to the unique flavor.
COCONUT: we used desiccated coconut unless otherwise specified.
Milk: available in cans from supermarkets.
Shredded: thin strips of dried coconut.
COINTREAU: orange-flavored liqueur.
CORNMEAL: ground corn (maize), pale yellow in color and fine. Yellow cornmeal is also available which is darker and coarser and is used in polenta. One cannot be substituted for the other as cooking times will vary.

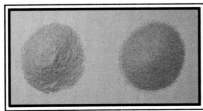
ABOVE: Cornmeal, yellow cornmeal.

COUSCOUS: a fine cereal made from semolina.
CREAM
Sour: a thick commercially cultured soured cream.
Whipping: is specified when necessary in recipes.
CSABAI: a type of Hungarian salami, available from most delicatessens.
CURRY POWDER: a combination of spices in powdered form. It consists of chili, coriander, cumin, fennel, fenugreek and turmeric in varying proportions.
CUSTARD POWDER: pudding mix.
DRIPPING: meat fat used as a shortening or for basting. Available from supermarkets.
FENNEL BULB: is eaten uncooked in salads or may be braised, steamed or stir-fried in savory dishes.
FISH: white cutlets, steaks, fillets.
Mullet: pinkish soft flesh, slightly oily.
Salmon: red-pink firm flesh; moist, delicate flavor; few bones.
Salt cod: dried salted cod, also known as baccala.
Smoked haddock: flesh is white with a mild smoky flavor; skin orange-colored.
Trout: round fish, moist firm flesh.
Tuna: reddish, firm flesh; slightly dry, no bones.
FISH SAUCE: an essential ingredient in the cooking of a number of South East Asian countries. It is made from the liquid drained from salted, fermented anchovies. It has a very strong smell and taste. Use sparingly until you acquire the taste.
FIVE-SPICE POWDER: a pungent mixture of ground spices which include cinnamon, cloves, fennel, star anise and Szechuan peppers.
FLOUR
Self-rising: substitute all-purpose flour and double-acting baking powder in the proportions of 1 cup all-purpose flour to 2 teaspoons double-acting baking powder. Sift together several times before using.
Whole-wheat self-rising: add baking powder to whole-wheat flour as above to make whole-wheat self-rising flour.
Buckwheat: triangular seeds, roasted and made into a flour used for pancakes and noodles.
GARAM MASALA: there are many variations of the combinations of cardamom, cinnamon, cloves, coriander, cumin and nutmeg used to make up this

ABOVE: Clockwise from front left: Red lentils, lima beans, yellow split peas, brown lentils, borlotti beans. Center: Haricot beans.

spice. Sometimes pepper is used to make a hot variation.

GHEE: a pure clarified butter fat available in cans, it can be heated to high temperatures without burning because of the lack of salts and milk solids.

GINGERROOT
Fresh or green: scrape away outside skin and grate, chop or slice as required.
Ground: is available but should not be substituted for fresh gingerroot in any recipe.

GRAND MARNIER: orange-flavored liqueur.

GREEN ONIONS: also known as scallions.

GREEN PEPPERCORNS: available in cans or jars, pickled in brine.

GUINEA HEN: a domestic and game bird very like pheasant.

HERBS: we have specified when to use fresh or dried herbs. We used dried (not ground) herbs in the proportion of 1:4 for fresh herbs; e.g., 1 teaspoon dried herbs instead of 4 teaspoons chopped fresh herbs.

HOISIN SAUCE: is a thick sweet Chinese barbeque sauce made from a mixture of salted black beans, onion and garlic.

HUMMUS: a paste of garbanzo beans, tahini (sesame paste), garlic, lemon juice and olive oil.

JUNIPER BERRIES: dried berries of an evergreen tree; juniper is the main flavoring ingredient in gin.

LAMB
Frenched rib chop: small, tender rib chop with fat trimmed from end of the bone.
Loin: row of chops from the mid-section.
Rack: row of rib chops.
Shank: portion of front or back leg with bone in.

LEEK: a member of the onion family, resembles the green onion but is much larger.

LEMON GRASS: available from Asian food stores; needs to be bruised or chopped before using.

LENTILS: there are many different types of lentils; they require overnight soaking or long cooking except for red lentils which are ready for cooking without soaking. See above. Brown lentils are red lentils from which the seedcoat has not been removed. See picture above.

MADEIRA: wine fortified with brandy.
MARSALA: a sweet fortified wine.
MORTADELLA: a delicately spiced and smoked cooked sausage made of pork and beef.

MUSHROOMS
Button: small, unopened mushrooms with a delicate flavor.
Dried Chinese: unique in flavor. Place mushrooms in bowl, cover with boiling water, stand 20 minutes; drain mushrooms, discard stems, use caps as indicated in recipes.
Flat: large, soft, flat mushrooms with a rich earthy flavor.
Straw: cultivated Chinese mushrooms about the size and shape of a quail egg, cream at the base and grey-black on top. Flavor is earthy. Sold canned in water.

ABOVE: Clockwise from left: dried Chinese mushrooms, button mushrooms, straw mushrooms.

MUSTARD, SEEDED: a French-style mustard with crushed mustard seeds.
OIL: polyunsaturated vegetable oil.
Olive: virgin oil is obtained only from the pulp of high-grade fruit. Pure olive oil is pressed from the pulp and kernels of second grade olives. Extra virgin olive oil is the purest quality virgin oil.
OLIVE PASTE: is made from olives, olive oil, salt, vinegar and herbs.
ONION, RED: we used large purplish-red colored onions where specified.
PANCETTA: cured pork belly; bacon can be substituted.
PARSLEY, FLAT-LEAFED: also known as continental parsley or Italian parsley.
PEARL BARLEY: barley which has had most of its outer husk removed.
PEPPERONI: sausage made from ground pork and beef with added fat; flavored with ground hot red pepper.
PIMIENTOS: canned or bottled bell peppers.
PITA POCKET BREAD: 2-layered round flat bread, can be cut open to form a pocket for filling.
PLUM SAUCE: a dipping sauce which consists of plums preserved in vinegar, sweetened with sugar and flavored with chilies and spices.

PORK
Fat: selvedge fat from pork loin.
Loin: from pork middle.
Neck: sometimes called pork scotch, from foreloin of pork.
Smoked: sometimes called kasseler.
Spare ribs: cut from the pork belly.
PROSCIUTTO: uncooked, unsmoked ham cured in salt; ready to eat when bought.
PRUNES: whole dried plums with a dark, wrinkled appearance.
QUAIL: small game birds weighing from 8oz to 10oz.

RABBIT
Cutlets: rabbit legs.
Pieces: jointed rabbit.
READY ROLLED PUFF PASTRY: frozen sheets of puff pastry available from supermarkets.

RICE
Arborio: large round-grained rice especially suitable for risottos.
Basmati: similar appearance to long-grain rice with a fine aroma. Basmati rice should be washed thoroughly before being cooked.
Brown: natural whole grain; takes longer to cook than white rice.
White: is hulled and polished, can be short or long-grained.
Wild: from North America, but not a member of the rice family. It has a distinctive flavor.
ROCK CORNISH HEN: small bird weighing about ¾lb to 1lb.
SAFFRON: the most expensive of all spices; it is available in strands or ground form. Saffron is made from the dried stamens of the crocus flower. The quality of this spice varies greatly.

SALAD LEAVES: we use mostly romaine lettuce, chicory, red leaf lettuce, radicchio and lollo rosso.

SAMBAL OELEK: (also ulek and olek) a paste made from ground chilies and salt.

SEASONED PEPPER: a combination of pepper, red bell pepper, garlic flakes, paprika and natural chicken extract.

SESAME OIL: made from roasted, crushed white sesame seeds and always used in small quantities. Do not use for frying.

SESAME SEEDS: there are 2 types, black and white; we used the white variety in this book. To toast: spread seeds evenly onto baking sheet, toast in 350°F oven for about 5 minutes.

SNOW PEAS: also known as Chinese pea pods.

SORREL: oval-shaped green leaves with bitter, slightly sour taste and a hint of lemon.

SOY SAUCE: made from fermented soy beans. The light sauce is generally used with white meat, and the darker variety with red meat. There is a multi-purpose salt-reduced sauce available, also Japanese soy sauce. It is personal taste which sauce you use.

SPECK: topside of leg of a mature pig, cut to shape and smoked. Use smoked bacon if unavailable.

SPINACH: a soft-leaved vegetable, more delicate in taste than Swiss chard; young Swiss chard can be substituted for spinach.

SPONGE FINGER COOKIES: available from most supermarkets.

SUET: hard white fat that surrounds the kidney in beef and mutton and is available from butchers.

SUGAR

We used coarse granulated table sugar, unless otherwise specified.

Dark Brown: a soft fine granulated sugar with molasses present which gives it its characteristic color.

SWEET POTATO: we used an orange-colored sweet potato.

SWISS CHARD: remove coarse white stems, cook green leafy parts as required by recipes.

TABASCO SAUCE: made with vinegar, hot red peppers and salt. Use in drops.

TAMARILLO: oval fruit with burgundy or yellow skin; has red flesh and tangy flavored seeds.

TOFU: made from boiled, crushed soy beans to give a type of milk. A coagulant is added, much like the process of cheese making. We used firm tofu in this book. Make sure you buy it as fresh as possible, keep any leftover tofu in the refrigerator under water, which must be changed daily.

TRIPE, HONEYCOMB: tripe comes from the first and second stomach of oxen; the latter is honeycomb. Tripe is sold cleaned, washed and blanched.

VEAL: the meat from dairy calves about 3 months of age.

Knuckle: the end of the leg, used for stewing.

Rib chops: from the neck end of the loin.

Shanks: osso bucco.

Shoulder: can be boned and rolled and roasted or cut up for stews.

VENISON: the meat of any animal from the deer family.

VINDALOO PASTE: thick, Indian seasoning paste with sour-hot flavor. Ingredients are ground chilies, coriander, cumin, fenugreek, mustard, fennel, cinnamon and cloves in a vinegar base.

VINEGAR: we used both white and brown (malt) vinegar in this book.

Balsamic: originated in the province of Modena, Italy. Regional wine is specially processed then aged in antique wooden casks to give pungent flavor.

WATER CHESTNUTS: small white crisp bulbs with a brown skin. Canned water chestnuts are peeled and will keep for about a month in the refrigerator.

WHEATGERM: small creamy flakes milled from the embryo of the wheat grain.

WHEATMEAL: ground wheat grains.

WINE: we used good-quality dry white and red wines.

WORCESTERSHIRE SAUCE: is a spicy sauce used mainly on red meat.

YELLOW SPLIT PEAS: dried peas suitable for purees and soups. Require soaking before cooking. See picture on page 124.

YOGURT: plain, unflavored yogurt is used as a meat tenderiser, enricher, thickener and also as a dessert ingredient.

MAKE YOUR OWN BROTH

BEEF BROTH

4lb meaty beef bones
2 onions
2 stalks celery, chopped
2 carrots, chopped
3 bay leaves
2 teaspoons black peppercorns
20 cups water
12 cups water, extra

Place bones and unpeeled chopped onions in roasting pan. Bake, uncovered, in 400°F oven about 1 hour or until bones and onions are well browned. Transfer bones and onions to large pan, add celery, carrots, bay leaves, peppercorns and water, simmer, uncovered, 3 hours. Add extra water, simmer, uncovered, further 1 hour; strain.

Makes about 10 cups.

■ Broth can be made 4 days ahead.
■ Storage: Covered, in refrigerator.
■ Freeze: Suitable.
■ Microwave: Not suitable.

CHICKEN BROTH

4lb chicken bones
2 onions, chopped
2 stalks celery, chopped
2 carrots, chopped
3 bay leaves
2 teaspoons black peppercorns
20 cups water

Combine all ingredients in large pan, simmer, uncovered, 2 hours; strain.

Makes about 10 cups.

■ Broth can be made 4 days ahead.
■ Storage: Covered, in refrigerator.
■ Freeze: Suitable.
■ Microwave: Not suitable.

FISH BROTH

3lb fish bones
12 cups water
1 onion, chopped
2 stalks celery, chopped
2 bay leaves
1 teaspoon black peppercorns

Combine all ingredients in large pan, simmer, uncovered, 20 minutes; strain.

Makes about 10 cups.

■ Broth can be made 4 days ahead.
■ Storage: Covered, in refrigerator.
■ Freeze: Suitable.
■ Microwave: Not suitable.

VEGETABLE BROTH

1 large carrot, chopped
1 large parsnip, chopped
2 onions, chopped
6 stalks celery, chopped
4 bay leaves
2 teaspoons black peppercorns
12 cups water

Combine all ingredients in large pan, simmer, uncovered, 1½ hours; strain.

Makes about 5 cups.

■ Broth can be made 4 days ahead.
■ Storage: Covered, in refrigerator.
■ Freeze: Suitable.
■ Microwave: Not suitable.

Index

CUP & SPOON MEASURES

To ensure accuracy in your recipes use standard measuring equipment.

a) 8 fluid oz cup for measuring liquids.
b) a graduated set of four cups – measuring 1 cup, half, third and quarter cup – for items such as flour, sugar, etc.
When measuring in these fractional cups level off at the brim.
c) a graduated set of five spoons: tablespoon (½ fluid oz liquid capacity), teaspoon, half, quarter and eighth teaspoons.
All spoon measurements are level.

We have used large eggs with an average weight of 2oz each in all our recipes.

Home Library

Salads

Sensational recipes for all occasions

Home Library

COUNTRY COOKING

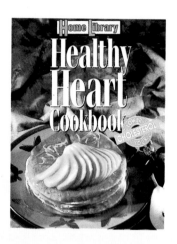

Home Library

Healthy Heart Cookbook

LOWER CHOLESTEROL EATING

Home Library

VEGETARIAN COOKING

THE BEST

Home Library

SEAFOOD RECIPES

Home Library

Italian COOKING CLASS COOKBOOK

Home Library

CHICKEN COOKBOOK

PLUS duck, quail, turkey, goose and more

Home Library

PASTA COOKBOOK

More than 170 recipes

Home Library

CHINESE COOKING CLASS COOKBOOK

Home Library

STARTERS AND SOUPS

Home Library

BEGINNERS' COOKBOOK

Home Library

FINGER FOOD

Best ever party food
Tempting hot and cold savouries
Do ahead and freezing tips